The
Visual Revolution Guidebook

How to build the skills you need for success in the new visual economy

Roz Morris

The Visual Revolution Guidebook
ISBN 978-1-915483-46-1 (paperback)
ISBN 978-1-915483-47-8 (ebook)

Published in 2024 by Right Book Press
Printed in the UK

© Roz Morris 2024

The right of Roz Morris to be identified as the author of this work has been asserted in accordance with the Copyright, Designs and Patents Act 1988.

A CIP record of this book is available from the British Library.

All rights reserved. No part of this book may be reproduced, stored in a retrieval system, or transmitted in any form or by any means, electronic, mechanical, photocopying, recording or otherwise, without the prior written permission of the copyright holder.

Contents

Introduction 1

1. How to make impactful videos on your phone 7
2. Looking professional online for meetings, presentations and interviews 19
3. Why appearance matters 35
4. Making the most of your presentations 47
5. How to appear confident in media interviews 71
6. How to handle difficult questions 95
7. How to handle documentary interviews 109
8. The power of podcasting 123
9. Building your profile online using free or inexpensive media 137
10. A glimpse into the metaverse 169
11. The future of the visual economy 181

Acknowledgements 187
Resources 189
About the author 201

Introduction

Why it pays to take the visual economy seriously

Like it or not, we're all living in a visual economy. Until the start of the 21st century, reading and writing dominated professional communications in industrialised societies. But now, businesses, governments, police forces, terrorist groups and even the British royal family make announcements in videos on social media. New developments in leisure and communications such as the growth of gaming and the metaverse are visual and there have never been so many tools available for creating visually appealing graphic designs for presentations and marketing. We are in the middle of a visual revolution which demands new skills from everyone in business and professional life.

It was the invention of writing thousands of years ago and subsequently of printing several hundred years ago that created the text economy – but now we're rapidly moving away from the domination of text in everyday communications. The introduction of universal education for children and the reduction of illiteracy in Europe in the 19th century was a response to the need for literate workers to be the clerks who provided the administration for businesses and governments. Until relatively recently, passing written exams with neat handwriting was seen as essential for career success. These days, reading and writing skills are no longer enough: visual literacy is equally important.

The digital revolution

The first mobile phones with built-in digital cameras were produced in 2000 by Sharp and Samsung. Since then, everything has changed. Anyone with a smartphone has the means to create text, images and videos and send them out into the world within seconds. This has put visual power into the hands of billions of people across the globe. According to a report by Exploding Topics, in 2023 it was estimated that there were approximately 6.5 billion smartphones in the world and that a majority of the global population of 8 billion owns at least one smartphone (Howarth 2023).

Marketing online now involves video, so the ability to talk to camera on social media is key. Facebook founder and Meta CEO and chairman Mark Zuckerberg correctly predicted all of this in 2016 when he told the Mobile World Congress in Barcelona, 'Most of the content ten years ago was text, and then photos, and now it's quickly becoming videos. I just think that we're going to be in a world a few years from now where the vast majority of the content that people consume online will be video.' The numbers back him up. Online video accounted for 60 per cent of all web traffic in 2013, rose to more than 80 per cent ten years later – and it's still going up (Feldman 2016).

The visual revolution

Across the world, the use of visual communication is constantly growing. We're increasingly communicating with static images and videos as well as text. We're using emojis instead of words. We're sending videos and memes when sharing our reactions to events. We're using avatars to play games in the metaverse. We can produce sophisticated graphics for our presentations without the need for a professional graphic designer.

My late father was a graphic designer who had precise skills – using paper, glue, pen, pencil, ruler, eraser, compasses and watercolour paints – which took him years to acquire. These skills are no longer necessary in the business world because tools to create images are now readily available on computers everywhere. We can create a visual impact in minutes and use this to get our ideas across to our friends, colleagues, clients or supporters. We can spend all day watching videos online and taking in vast amounts of visual information as well as reading subtitles. AI technology is increasing the ease and speed with which we can produce videos and images. Yes, we still need to read, but the visual economy is a huge part of our everyday lives. This means we need visual skills as part of our everyday skillsets. If you want to enjoy success in your career, reading and writing skills are no longer enough. It's vital to understand the grammar of the visual economy and this book sets out what you need to know to rise above amateurism and be professional in all your visual communications.

My media story

I was a product of the text economy and have worked in the media for my entire adult life. I read History at Oxford University, discovered that I liked writing for *Cherwell*, the university's student newspaper and gained a traineeship as a newspaper reporter on *The Guardian*. After three years of typing up my copy and handing it in on paper or phoning it in using landlines in offices or public phone boxes, I changed from daily news to the Sunday newspaper, *The Observer*, and kept on typing up or phoning in my copy. This was long before mobiles existed and even before faxes were widely used!

I moved on to BBC radio reporting, then worked as a TV reporter for the BBC, ITV News and RTE, the Irish state broadcaster, for whom I was a London correspondent. At different times I was based in cities including London, Manchester, Newcastle upon Tyne and Edinburgh, covering news stories all around the UK and abroad. I learned how to use a lot of different technologies, including manual, electric and electronic typewriters, computers, reel-to-reel tape recorders and cassette recorders, and how to write scripts and edit reports for radio and television news using taped audio and video. Then I learned how to use digital technologies.

The media industry has always adapted to new technologies but in the 21st century the tools that used to belong only to print, radio and TV journalists, camera operators, editors and producers have become available to all. Graphic design and printing are easily accessible on every office computer and the days when all these media skills were separate and required different jobs with specialist training are long gone. When I was a young

Introduction

newspaper journalist in the 1970s, print workers were highly unionised and if any journalist even accidentally touched any machinery, the printers would come out on a work to rule or even go on strike. When I moved on to radio reporting for the BBC, at least I was able to edit my own reports and could move fast to get reports on the air despite the heavy tape recorders we had to use.

Moving into television reporting, I caught the tail end of the use of film for news reports. The film crew for Thames News, then London's local TV station, included a director, a production assistant, a cameraman and assistant cameraman, a sound recordist and assistant sound recordist, a lighting technician and assistant, and three drivers to take us to filming locations in three cars! The crew belonged to several different trade unions and sometimes one or two of the unions would be on a work to rule, so their hours and duties were restricted. Cans of film had to be sent for processing and then brought back to the newsroom an hour or so later for editing by another set of skilled people, the film editors. The whole laborious process meant it could take all day to produce one short news report. And I haven't even mentioned the cumbersome ways of recording the voiceover or adding captions, all of which can be done far more swiftly and easily using digital software.

I'd always wanted to be a TV news reporter but this restrictive system for TV news production came as a big shock. I told my friends, 'I feel as though I've finally qualified to run in the Olympics, but the organisers have tied bricks to my ankles.' Things speeded up when we moved on to using videotapes for news with smaller news crews, but this was still painfully slow compared to today's instant smartphone videos. I acquired a lot of visual skills as a TV reporter and presenter and went on to set up my own media training company, TV News London Ltd, to help people working in business and the professions, in politics, in universities, in charities and many other walks of life, to deliver TV and radio interviews professionally. No matter what the technology, the skills of communicating the spoken word clearly and looking convincing while you do this need to be learned. The arrival of the visual economy means that skills that used to belong only to the few now need to be universal.

How to use this book

You don't need to read this book in any particular order. Each chapter deals with the different challenges and demands created by the visual economy. There is expert advice on making videos, taking selfies, personal branding, using social media, giving media interviews, avoiding mistakes with your appearance, setting up your own podcast or being interviewed on someone else's. There is advice on taking part in documentaries, becoming an influencer, spotting deepfakes and information on the metaverse and how it's already being used by a variety of different businesses and organisations. The visual economy is fascinating and there's a lot to learn if you want to succeed in it.

Why I've written this book

I'm passionate about clear communication, looking professional and levelling the playing field to help people from all walks of life do their best in the visual economy. As a broadcaster, writer and media trainer with many years of experience, I want to share my knowledge of the skills you need to succeed in the visual economy. Visual media skills are now regular business skills, and this book will help you to develop yours. So, let's get started.

Chapter 1

How to make impactful videos on your phone

The popularity of short-form video has soared in the past few years with the rise of TikTok and the introduction of YouTube Shorts and Instagram Reels. This huge growth in the number of people talking to camera on social media means there's a need for ever larger numbers of spokespeople to be able to deliver effective videos in a wide variety of settings. LinkedIn reports that video drives five times more engagement than any other type of content and generates 20 more shares. These developments mean that TV and radio communication skills are now essential business skills. But presenting a cat or a funny baby video doesn't qualify you to present a business video. When you make videos on your phone you need to know how to avoid common mistakes.

If you have a small business, you can post videos on your company website and then put posts on all of your business-related social media. You can use your videos to establish your own YouTube or Vimeo channel and post advice videos with sales information as well as purely sales videos. You can also post short videos with your mailings to clients and potential clients. There's free advice available on YouTube and Vimeo about how to upload videos and how to make videos for ads, and Google Ads also has advice on how to run ad campaigns using video.

The cheapest and simplest way to make your own videos is to use your smartphone. You can be conversational and look casual if it suits your message – but don't be fooled into thinking your videos will just effortlessly happen. There's plenty of help and advice available online but you have to work at it. You can use the tools on Vimeo and sign up for free trials of their video services or you can subscribe to the YouTube Creators channel for the latest news tips and updates. It isn't hard to upload your videos once you have made them but you need to be sure that they look competent before you do that. Here are my tips for making the best videos and how to avoid common mistakes.

Content

First, establish your goal and your messages. Do you want to make a video advertising specific, time-limited products or services? Or do you want to make a classic advice video that won't go out of date? Keep your content concise and conversational. If you want to demonstrate your expertise, less is more. Keep it short and your shots simple. For the most basic video messages, you only need one shot. Look at other short business videos online and work out what you want to do based on those that have the most views. One-minute videos work well on LinkedIn and other social media platforms.

Rehearse

The first and most important point about making your own videos is that you need time to rehearse. Professional TV presenters always rehearse before going for a take. This means you need to run through your content and figure out how and where you will stand or sit to deliver it. Don't be a one-take wonder. You should expect to do several takes and only send out the best one. If you're worried about being on video, just remember that you'll improve with practice. You can't learn to swim without getting in the pool and you can't learn to make videos without getting in front of a camera. Just do it.

Voice

The tone and pitch of your voice are important, so rehearsal is essential. Speaking in a monotone is not acceptable – make sure you vary your tone and pace. You're talking to people, so be upbeat and engaging.

Face

It's hard to smile when you're concentrating on content or you're not used to talking to camera but you need to figure out what sort of smiling suits you. Wide grins don't work for everyone. Sometimes it's better to look and sound positive and helpful. If you need to appear concerned as you outline the problem you're going to solve for people, you need to work on that as well. Getting your facial expressions right will take practice.

How to avoid common video mistakes

Don't make too many points: Keep your message short and concise and don't make more than three points. If you have six thoughts to offer, you can make two or even three videos.

Use landscape shots: Using the landscape setting means that you'll fill the screen and won't have black strips at each side of the video. Portrait shots are OK for funny cat, dog and baby videos but are not so useful for business content on LinkedIn or YouTube ads. However, YouTube shorts, TikTok and other 'younger' social media platforms expect portrait shots. Check before you create your content.

Always check your camera angle: ensure you're not cutting off your head or positioning yourself too high or too low in your shot.

Check your technical settings: Use the highest possible setting on your smartphone, either HD, UHD or 4K and for filming use the MP4 format.

Use the rule of thirds: Check the grid boxes on the screen and place yourself in the middle of your shot. This is the way that professional photographers and videographers frame their shots. The rule of thirds is a rule of thumb often used to place a subject at an intersection of the lines in a three by three grid – this creates more interest and leaves the rest of the scene more open.

Use a tripod: Don't expect to be able to hold your phone without wobbling, which will make your audience feel a bit seasick. You can stabilise your phone by placing it against books or a cushion but you'll do better with a tripod. Buy a small tripod online; the ones with bendy legs are very adaptable.

Don't forget to keep still: Keep your framing tight in a medium close-up. A moving picture is harder to watch and stay focused on. If you move around, your audience might stop listening to you. Also, it takes skill to move while remembering what you want to say and not jerking the phone around. Many videos on YouTube and Vimeo that show people walking and talking are shot using a camera operator with a video camera, not a smartphone. They can also use a camera with a gimbal so the picture remains steady while moving about.

Check your eyeline: Eyeline is important. If you're talking direct to camera, keep your eyes on the camera throughout the time you're talking. Avoid looking to one side or the other, or up and down. Don't flick your eyes from side to side either. This will puzzle your audience and make you appear nervous. Train yourself to keep your eyes on the camera. Set up your phone level with your face and remember that when you're talking your head can go down, so always keep your shoulders back and your head up.

Use the interview format: If you're nervous or unsure about talking direct to camera, you could use an interview format, with an interviewer sitting just out of shot to one side of you. The audience doesn't need to see the interviewer or hear their questions but, because you're looking off camera, it will be obvious that you're talking to an interviewer and this can pique interest. What else did you say in your interview? You can use quotes from the interview in subsequent posts or use this format for short adverts. You may find it easier to get your points across in this format than if you talk directly to the camera but remember to keep your eyeline steady and look at the interviewer throughout.

Count your words like a broadcaster: Follow the technique that broadcasters use to get their timings right. When broadcasters are writing scripts for news reports they count three words a second. This means that broadcasters speak at 180 words per minute, which is quite a brisk pace; 180 words divided by three words per second gives you 60 seconds. So, if you're recording a one-minute video, you should aim for around 160 to 180 words.

Stay silent and remain still at the beginning and the end: It's essential to leave clear gaps with no sound at the beginning and end of your videos. Broadcasters always do this. Here's how. Start recording and stay silent. Look into your camera while slowly counting down in your head, '5, 4, 3, 2, 1'. Then breathe in and speak. Make your points, introduce yourself and include a call to action. What do you want your audience to do? At the end, stop speaking and smile. Stay silent and count down '5, 4, 3, 2, 1' before you move or stop the recording.

Light your video location: Choose a location with good, even light. Avoid a room or a place that's too dark, too light or half lit and half dark. You might think that if you go upstairs to your loft office, you'll have lots of light, but there can be problems with lighting in a loft. Sitting under a roof window through which light is streaming can look strange, especially if you have a blob of bright light on the top of your head. You may need to pull the blind down and use other lighting. You can diffuse some sunlight by pulling net curtains across a window to make the light softer. To ensure that your lighting is even wherever you're sitting, it's a good idea to invest in a ring light. You can put this on a stand or a small desk tripod. These have been used by professional fashion and beauty photographers for many years but are now in common use for videos and online meetings because they minimise shadows and soften and enhance the quality of the face. In short, they provide a more flattering and professional-looking shot. A ring light is easy to use and easy to order online. However, it's best to avoid the cheapest ones as they tend not to last very long. You can shoot through the middle of the ring light or combine it with daylight and have it to one side of your shot. You can experiment to get this right. You can get help on this by viewing some of the many YouTube videos with advice on using ring lights. Evening lighting can be a problem, so adjust it to work for you. Make sure your room lights aren't too harsh and creating unflattering shadows. My advice would be to avoid shooting your videos in the evening as it's much more difficult to get your lighting right.

Do a sound check: You can use the built-in microphone on your smartphone to make videos but it picks up all the sound around it, which means the sound quality on your videos may suffer. I'd recommend investing in a cardioid microphone. This is a type of directional microphone that's designed to pick up sound primarily from one direction while minimising background noise from other directions. It will provide better-quality voice recordings than the omnidirectional microphone on your phone. When filming videos, it's better not to hold a microphone in your hand. You can easily purchase a lapel microphone, also known as a lavalier, or lav mic, which you clip onto your clothes, close to your mouth. These mics can be plugged into your phone or you can use a wireless one.

Check your background and location: Your background shouldn't be too busy or feature lots of images; nor should you have people moving around behind you. If your audience has to decode too much visual information, they won't be paying full attention and may drift away entirely. Ideally you should choose a location with little or no background noise. Don't be tempted to try recording in a coffee shop or on a busy road, as your audience won't be able to take in what you're saying. You may think your location isn't that noisy. However, our ears filter out background noise but microphones don't – they just record everything. Your sound will be messy and you'll be hard to understand if there's a lot of background noise.

Keep your outfit plain and simple: Unless you're promoting a fashion brand, it's best to keep your clothes plain and simple. Never wear anything that looks tight, crumpled or shiny. You can be casual but not scruffy. Avoid tiny patterns that can strobe on-screen. Large patterns can also be distracting. There's more advice on what to wear on-screen in Chapter 4.

Check your captions and subtitles: Many business videos make it look simple but, if you want to use captions and subtitles, you have to ensure they're correct. There are numerous systems on offer, some much more effective than others. As a beginner you can try the YouTube Create app, which lets you edit videos on your phone free of charge. Vimeo also offers free as well as paid services. Other subtitling offers include Adobe Premier Pro, VEED.io, Subtitle Bee and Caption Me.

You can do all of this yourself or you can shoot your video and hand it over to professional editors. Karen Pawlowska, founder and managing director of Take One TV, is a subtitles expert. She used to run the BBC Subtitling Unit; when she worked on the children's TV programme *Blue Peter*, she was part of a team that pioneered the use of subtitles on the BBC. She now runs her own video production company and has made hundreds of business videos. Her advice is to always take care over your captions and subtitles. She says: 'Many people don't turn the sound up on videos and just read the subtitles, so it's important to have subtitles and not to show anything inaccurate or that doesn't make sense. There's an art to subtitling. You don't have to do it word for word but you do have to get a lot of info in. You have to work out how long a subtitle should be on-screen without it being too fast for people to read. The main meaning of messages must always be conveyed clearly, so take the time to get this right. You can use AI to provide subtitling but it does need to be checked for accuracy.'

Take one extra shot: If you hire a video producer to edit your videos, Karen's advice is to take a screenshot of your business card so that the video editor has the correct spelling of your name and job title. You don't want to end up paying for extra editing time because your name caption is incorrect.

Promote your videos: Once you've created your videos, you have valuable assets that you can use for your marketing. You can use them in mailings, on social media, on your website, on YouTube and Vimeo, in online ads and in your presentations.

Consider AI: There's no doubt that AI is a game changer in the world of video production. Producers are using AI to create storyboards, shot lists, call sheets, shooting schedules, captions, subtitles, and to write draft scripts. AI can look for locations, investigate film permits and research stock footage. Using AI can hugely reduce the time required for both the creative and the production process and it can whizz through time-consuming tasks in seconds. If you're making short videos on your smartphone, you won't need to take on all the processes and tasks required for longer videos. However, you can use AI to edit your videos and upload them. You can start off with the free version of ChatGPT, which offers simple trimming and video editing, then decide whether you want to pay for the more sophisticated version; similarly with Vimeo, YouTube and Google Gemini. To create images using AI, you could start with Microsoft Bing's Image Creator and for realistic AI-generated voices, check out Eleven Labs.

To produce videos explaining new services or showcasing products, you can use AI video generation tools – these include InVideo, Pictory and RawShorts and have templates and tools for AI-generated voiceovers, avatars, animations and footage. If it suits your brand, you can create your own avatar – your digital twin – so that you always look smart and exactly the same in all your videos. You record your voice, and AI will use it to voice your scripts. TikTok Stories has Speechify Studio, which provides you with AI narrators for your videos. If you prefer to stick to the real you, RawShorts, InVideo, Canva and Pictory all have AI-powered options for social media video creation. The choice is yours.

How much AI is good for your brand?

Think carefully about using AI avatars. Using AI for video production can save time but you have to decide how much you need to maintain a personal and human touch in your videos. AI should enhance, not replace, the personal connection between your brand and your audience. Except for basic instructional videos, humans mostly want humans to talk to them and convince them to buy. AI can provide tremendous benefits, but it does have to be checked for inaccuracies. AI experts talk of the necessity for 'improving factuality' and call this 'hallucinating'. If a large language model (LLM) can't find the data that enables it to answer a specific question, it will fabricate a result and even create a fictitious research paper, citing a publication that doesn't exist.

So, while AI can give you a draft script for your video, you must always check it thoroughly. Never assume it's 100 per cent accurate. You should also check any images AI creates for you. For example, if you write your prompt and ask AI to produce an image of someone on the phone in an office, it can give you a picture that looks realistic except that the landline phone might have a cable that goes straight into a desk and the person holding the handset has six fingers or an extra thumb.

AI is constantly improving so these problems are diminishing. The secret of success is making sure your prompts are detailed and specific, or you can end up with images that look odd and unconvincing. AI videos can be useful for educational and instructional videos, but you have to decide whether this is appropriate for you and your business. Will you be better off sticking to videos with real people? If your answer is yes, I've found that most people benefit greatly from training in presenting videos so they can develop their online presenting skills, build their confidence, and be sure they're not making any obvious mistakes.

Chapter 2

Looking professional online for meetings, presentations and interviews

Before the Covid-19 pandemic, it wasn't unknown for people to have meetings or training sessions online – but it was unusual. In the five years before 2020, I ran just a handful of online media training sessions. These were mostly on Skype and were all for clients based outside the UK. Everything changed after the first UK lockdown began in March 2020. It meant no face-to-face meetings for office workers and no in-person media and presentation training courses for me and my colleagues. Suddenly, like many people across the world, I was working on Zoom, Teams or other video conferencing platforms. It was a culture shock that brought new and unexpected challenges in terms of maintaining professional standards at meetings and in media interviews and WFH (working from home) became a common abbreviation. As one commentator memorably observed, we all began seeing an awful lot of other people's bookcases, kitchens and even bedrooms.

Too many people are badly lit

I was struck by the fact that I'd never seen so many badly lit people. This occurred both at online meetings and on TV, where spokespeople were talking from their homes instead of TV studios. As well as sitting in the dark, many people were looking in the wrong direction, some were out of focus, some were too small, some too large on-screen and even more were looking a bit scruffy. And then it hit me. Too many people are thinking that an online business meeting is like a phone call. But it isn't. It's an on-screen performance that requires the skills of a broadcaster. This mistake was true for many people when we all started doing interviews and meetings online. Sadly, you can still see people getting this wrong and I always advise clients to check their online settings both at home and at work to ensure they have a professional image on-screen.

Your seven steps to visual success online

During the lockdowns, I soon realised that we're all broadcasters now. But we're not just presenters. WFH means we have to be the producer and director as well as the presenter. So, I started offering clients my expert advice on how to look good online and explaining my seven steps to success in webinars. Clients found this really valuable and built it into their reputation management policies.

Here's the checklist for your seven steps to visual success online. Always check the following:

1. Background

Is it too 'busy'? Will your audience spend more time looking at what's behind you rather than listening to what you say? Check for the following potential distractions and remove them wherever possible.

- **Bookcases:** If you're sitting in front of a bookcase, is it tidy? Will people mentally start tidying it up? Can people read some of the titles and be distracted by thinking about them?
- **Family photos:** These can be distracting in meetings and especially in media interviews. People can't help looking at photos and trying to understand and process them. It's best to remove them from the shot.
- **Posters and paintings:** Whether they're behind you or to the side, people can't ignore posters and paintings. But while they're deciphering them they aren't concentrating on what you're saying.
- **Kitchens:** If you're not selling kitchens, kitchen equipment, cookery books or promoting a restaurant, why are you sitting in a kitchen? Consider whether this is an appropriate background for your interview or meeting. If you have to use your kitchen for online interviews or meetings, make sure it's tidy and uncluttered.
- **Bedrooms:** If you have to use a bedroom for your interview or meeting, make sure that people can't see that it's a bedroom, otherwise you run the risk of people feeling as if they're intruding into your private life. Or they may start thinking about your style of bedroom, your headboard, your bed linen and so on. It's an absolute no-no to have a visibly

unmade bed but it's best to avoid having a bed in the background at all. If your home office desk is in a bedroom, sit with a blank wall behind you.

+ **Offices:** When you're using an office for interviews, always check the background as advised above. It's sensible to have a plain background and avoid messy scribbles on whiteboards and untidy piles of papers. If objects in the background are puzzling your viewers, they may never really listen to what you're saying. Avoid sitting in front of large plants as they may look as if they're growing out of your head. The same warning applies to Christmas trees. Always use an office or meeting room with a door that locks and stick a 'do not disturb' notice on the outside.

+ **Open-plan offices:** These are not suitable for online meetings and interviews. They're usually too noisy for giving interviews and can have too many people moving about in the background. If you conduct a live TV or radio interview in an open-plan office, you won't be able to eliminate the possibility that someone in the office may not realise you're giving an interview or are in a meeting and they may interrupt you by loudly asking if you'll be coming to the pub after work or, even worse, swearing or delivering a rude joke.

Case study: Angela Terry

Yes, it's true – a picture really is more powerful than a thousand words. At the beginning of 2022, Angela Terry, an environmental scientist from Somerset faced a storm of criticism when she chose to do an interview on the ITV show *Good Morning Britain* about new government regulations that will make it more difficult for UK housebuilders to justify building conservatories in new homes. The problem was that she delivered a message about climate change while sitting in her own conservatory. She was accused of hypocrisy by her interviewers and in reports in newspapers and online. The image took over the story and Mail Online jumped in with the headline 'People in glass houses! Green campaigner lectures GMB viewers on damage that conservatories are doing to the planet – while sitting in her conservatory' (Gant 2022). There were many hostile comments on what was then Twitter, including memes questioning Ms Terry's intelligence and comments asking why, if she was so worried about conservatories, did she buy a house that had one?

This example proves the rule that image dominates on TV, on video, on social media and in online meetings. If you want to get your points across and remembered in a positive way, always look at your background and assess it critically. As Angela Terry found out, this could save you a lot of bother. Criticisms of her interview fed into the anti-green narrative portraying green campaigners as hypocrites. On the other hand, she did get a lot of publicity for the issue of conservatories contributing to global warming, so maybe sitting in her own conservatory to be interviewed wasn't such a poor decision after all!

Case study: The trouserless MEP

Early on in the 2020 lockdown, an Irish member of the European Parliament sat on his bed to take part in a session. This setting was entirely inappropriate for taking part in a formal debate and it was made even worse by the fact that he had failed to realise his bare legs were visible. He wasn't wearing any trousers and kept scratching his legs. Not surprisingly, he was roundly condemned for this lapse in online etiquette (Carroll 2020).

2. Lighting

Do you have too little or too much light on your face? Windows are not your friend. It's important to realise that natural light is not reliable in many parts of the world. You may start off being well lit and then be plunged into darkness. If you draw your curtains or blinds to avoid variations in light levels, you may end up in an eerie half-light that's very unflattering. To look professional, you need a reliable light source on your face. It's important not to sit in the dark or with too much light. When a window is to one side of you, you run the risk of having only one half of your face lit. This can look strange and puzzling to the audience. Never sit with a window behind you. If you do, you'll look odd because the window and your background will be lighter than you and your face may be in darkness. Being backlit like this is a big disadvantage. People don't like being unable to see the face of a speaker clearly. If you have to sit near a window, sit in front of it facing the window. Some people have their home office in a loft extension and often have a window above their head. This can cause problems because light can stream in on the top of the head, which looks odd and distracting. It's best to pull down the window blind when you're talking on-screen and use other lighting.

Invest in lighting you can rely on. To get regular light onto your face, put a table lamp or a ring light behind your computer screen pointing towards you or put table lamps on either side of your screen. The best way to avoid all these light hazards is to invest in a ring light that will give you an even, soft light on your face. When using your smartphone, use a portable ring light.

3. Framing

The rule of thirds is a simplified version of the Golden Ratio, which was used by artists for centuries to create classic compositions. It splits an image into thirds vertically and horizontally so that there are nine rectangles, as shown in the grids below. This is the same grid that you can use for photos and videos on smartphones and tablets. You should position your head in the top third of the screen and be far enough away to allow your shoulders and the tops of your arms to be seen.

The Visual Revolution Guidebook

Correct framing:

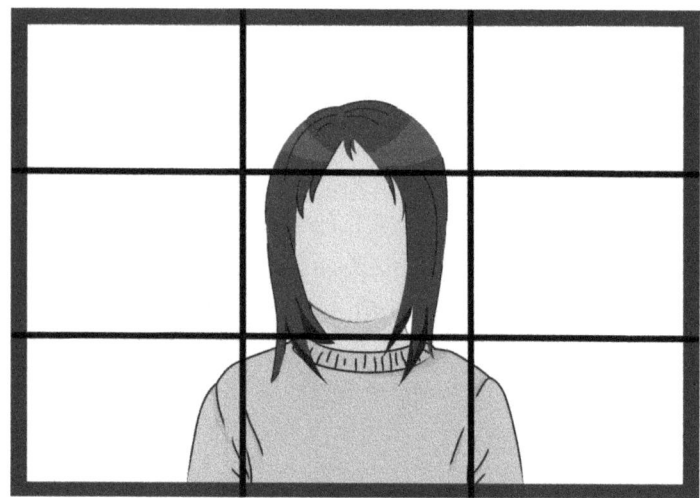

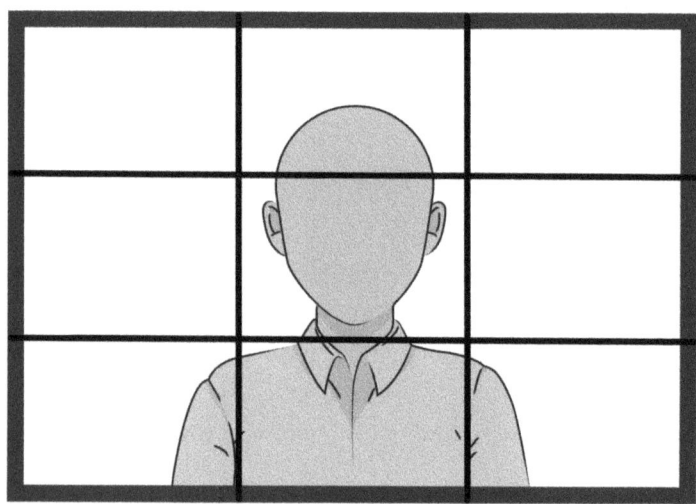

Incorrect framing:

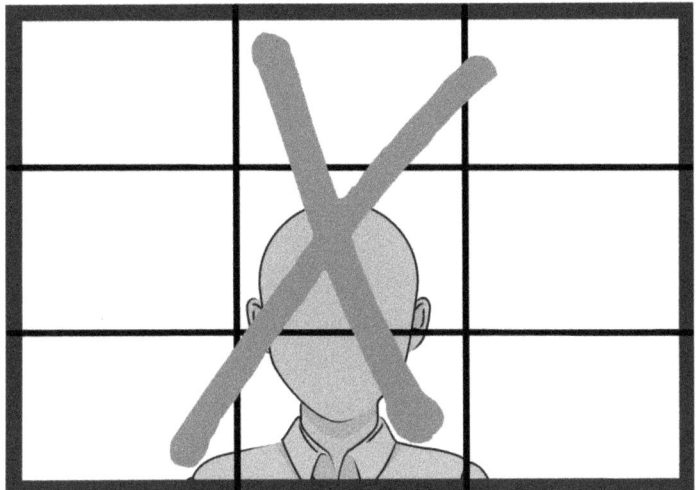

Avoid the following framing mistakes:

+ **Too low or too high:** You'll look odd and sloppy if you position yourself low down in the shot. You'll also look odd if you're too high up on the screen.
+ **Too close:** Don't get too close to the camera. This will look strange and feel a bit threatening to your audience. You also run the risk of being out of focus when you get too close to the lens.
+ **Too much to one side:** You shouldn't be appearing to the left or the right of the screen. In order to look 'normal', you should be in the middle of the screen. Symmetry works best when framing your shot.
+ **Looking down at your laptop or computer screen:** If you don't set up your laptop properly for online meetings or media interviews, it's easy to look a bit distorted with lots of ceiling dominating your shot. Never look down at your camera. Keep it level with

your eyes and talk to the camera rather than the images of people on the screen.
+ **Leaning:** Always sit up straight and don't lean to one side or the other. Leaning can make you look sloppy and undermine your authority.

4. Sound

Invest in a good-quality microphone (see Chapter 1). If your sound quality is poor during meetings, media interviews or job interviews, people will think you're not as competent as they have a right to expect. It can also irritate other people in your meeting if they can't hear you properly and have to ask you to repeat what you've said. If you're giving a media interview online, poor sound isn't going to make you come across as the expert that you are. Print, radio and TV interviews can all be conducted online, so getting your sound right is of everyday importance. Always check your sound levels before you start a meeting or an interview.

Case study: The Irish lecturers

> In December 2020, the president of the Galway and Mayo Institute of Technology (GMIT) in Ireland had to issue an apology following publicity about a student recording of two college lecturers who had switched off their cameras but not their audio at the end of a meeting. Their students then heard what their teachers *really* thought about them and their virtual presentations. One of the lecturers said, 'I thought I'd have to get a drill and start drilling my teeth, they were so painful to be listening to.' GMIT

> spent €5,000 on commissioning an independent report into this incident, which they called a 'very regrettable occurrence' and which led them to introduce staff and student training in the use of technology and communications (Deegan 2020).

5. Eyeline

Getting your eyeline right is important when it comes to giving you authority, whether in media interviews or meetings. There are a number of useful techniques to help you maintain eye contact with a camera throughout interviews and when you're speaking in meetings. Whatever the size of the camera lens, look at the top of the lens and then down by a third to gain the best eyeline for talking to camera. In media interviews you must keep your eyes on the camera throughout your interview. TV is an unforgiving medium and it can feel unnatural when it comes to keeping your eyes constantly on the camera. However, if you don't follow the rule on keeping your eyeline steadily on the camera and you look up, down or to the side during interviews, the audience will be wondering why you're looking in the wrong place. Most people will have no idea how hard it is to look at an interviewer or a camera for the entire time you're talking but they've all watched a lot of TV, and they'll always know when you're getting your eyeline wrong.

As I've pointed out before, we're all broadcasters now, so when you're speaking online, it's advisable to follow the same rules for meetings as you would for remote TV interviews when you talk direct to camera. When you're talking or presenting during business meetings, it's a good practice to keep your eyes on the camera, not on what else and who else is on your screen. You can vary your eyeline when you're not talking but when you start talking again you have to resist the temptation to speak to the image of the person who asked the question or who's chairing the meeting. This will make your eyeline look odd so you have to talk to the camera in order to look normal.

Looking straight at the camera feels unnatural but it looks natural on-screen. This is something you should practise until it becomes easy for you and you don't look strained or worried. You can practise this in online meetings so that you're ready to talk to camera in TV interviews. It's a good idea to watch TV news and see how people look nervous and unsure when their eyes are moving around.

If you're using an iPad, the camera is on one side for a landscape shot and this makes it harder to maintain a good eyeline. If you don't look at the camera, it will appear as if you're looking to the left of the screen. Your audience will find this distracting. They may not know how to do TV interviews professionally, but they do know that you should be looking at them. It's part of the unspoken grammar of TV that we're all brought up with. You can solve the problem by standing the iPad upright with the camera at the top and opting for a portrait shot. However, this has a couple of disadvantages. It will look as if you're on your phone and won't look as polished as a landscape shot. You'll also have wasted space either side of you on-screen. Portrait shots aren't suitable for interviews in a business setting.

6. Appearance

This issue is so important I've dedicated a chapter to it (see Chapter 3).

7. Avoid interruptions

If you're WFH, always make sure you have a quiet place to speak where no pets, children or other family members can interrupt you. Make sure everyone knows you're in a business meeting or giving a media interview. Some people have locked the door and family members have still knocked on it. You have to be firm with everyone before you go online. Stick a notice on the door telling people to keep out and not to knock.

You may remember Professor Robert Kelly, whose two children and his wife came into shot behind him while he was in the middle of an interview with *BBC News*. Most people don't remember what he was talking about. In fact, he was being interviewed about the impeachment of South Korea's former president Park Geun-hye and the political implications of this very serious issue. Unfortunately, his interview turned into a comedy classic that went viral (Usborne 2017). The video is good for a laugh, but this isn't what you want to happen when you're talking about a serious topic. Since Professor Kelly's interview went viral in 2017, we've had the Covid-19 lockdowns and interviews from home have become commonplace. Politicians and businesspeople have also been interrupted by small children, teenagers, cats and dogs while giving interviews online. More unusually, Sir Richard Branson had problems with insects. He found it hard to make himself heard during an interview with ITV's *Good Morning Britain* when he was speaking from Mallorca. He was talking about problems with UK air traffic control systems and also his own dyslexia, but viewers took to social media to point out that all they could hear were some extremely noisy crickets (O'Connor 2023). If you're not using your phone for your meeting/interview, put it in airplane mode or turn it off and leave it in another room. This is better than putting your phone on silent when it will still emit electrical pulses that can be picked up by microphones.

Case study: The naked wife

In South Africa, a local community leader was criticised for allowing his wife to walk into shot naked during an online committee meeting that was running late. It was reported that the chair of the meeting said this was the second time this had happened. The community leader said it was past his wife's bedtime and he didn't have another room to use (Baker 2021). Managing your family when you have late-night meetings can be problematic!

Case study: Airplane irony

After Alaska Airlines flight 1282 had an emergency door panel blowout at 16,000 feet in January 2024, an aviation expert who was being interviewed in the studio at *Sky News* was embarrassed when his phone rang three times. Comments on social media pointed out that it was ironic that he was discussing aviation but had forgotten to put his phone in airplane mode. Eventually the presenter took the phone away and gave it to a member of the crew to remove from the studio.

There have been numerous examples reported in the media about embarrassment caused by people forgetting to switch off their cameras at the end of meetings. They may swear or make inappropriate comments about colleagues, pick their noses or scratch themselves without realising they're still on camera. Some of the most staggering examples of careless behaviour during online meetings include a lawyer in Peru who was seen stripping off his clothes and having sex with a naked woman when he left his camera on during an online court hearing. In Canada and Argentina, members of parliament have had to resign after inappropriate behaviour during live parliamentary sessions. In Canada, an MP was seen coming out of his shower naked and in Argentina a married MP was seen kissing his girlfriend's breasts. Other careless Zoom users include a government official in the Philippines who was videoed having sex with his secretary after accidentally joining a meeting with his colleagues on a village council.

These may seem like extreme examples of bad behaviour online but it's important to recognise that all the examples in this chapter are reported on the internet and available to look up within seconds. So, if you do make a bad mistake, it won't go away and can live forever online as a reputation-damaging, career-sabotaging piece of information. Even if you leave your camera and microphone on and comment critically about colleagues, you can, at the very least, suffer embarrassment with your fellow workers. And beyond that, let's not forget the friends they send your mistake to, the bosses they report you to and the future employers who won't employ you because your story gets picked up and used by journalists, who are always looking for online blunders to write about.

Chapter 3

Why appearance matters

When you're recording a video, giving a presentation or a media interview, whether online or in person, appearance really matters. As part of your preparation for an interview or a presentation, it's important to give some detailed thought to your appearance. This isn't about vanity; it's about being practical and should always form part of your preparation for meetings and interviews.

Case study: Lord Heseltine

> When I interviewed former British deputy prime minister Lord Heseltine for a corporate video, I was struck by how much care he took over his appearance. He had many years of experience of giving interviews for both TV news and videos, so he knew exactly what to do when he was told we were ready to start the interview. We were at his company headquarters and had set up the cameras and lighting in the boardroom next to his office. Before entering the room, he combed his hair and made sure it was tidy. Then he brushed his

shoulders to remove any hairs and undid his jacket so it wouldn't bunch up when he sat down. He does all of this as a matter of routine and as a result has always looked smart on-screen. He wears a suit and tie for political or business interviews but when talking about his estate and large garden, he wears a smart jumper with a shirt and no tie. He has never looked scruffy, unkempt or unsuitably dressed.

Clothing choices can cause problems

It used to be that only women giving TV interviews had to worry about the extensive choice of clothing available to them; men just wore suits and ties. Now a smart casual look can be acceptable for men, so there are far more choices for them too. Women can wear dresses or smart tops and trousers, with or without a jacket, and look smart – provided they stick to the rules on avoiding patterns. Things became more difficult for men about 15 years ago when David Cameron, as UK leader of the opposition, ushered in the trend (which he later abandoned) of not wearing a tie for his TV and public appearances. Many men found out that this look is a lot harder to pull off than it looks. See the clothing advice lists later in this chapter.

Patterns can also cause problems

Whether you wear smart casual or smart clothes, it's best to avoid large or small patterns, including dots, spots, stripes and tweeds. Frills, asymmetrical clothes and large pieces of jewellery are also distracting for your audience.

Large patterns can be distracting because people will focus on them and try to work out what they are. Flowers? What type of flowers? Or are those leaves? What do these swirly patterns mean? Even worse – is that really a cat crawling out of that T-shirt? Small patterns can create problems because cameras can't always cope with tiny colour changes, so dots, spots and stripes can cause the picture to strobe – which means moving about, looking as if it's vibrating. Tweeds often have very small patterns and colour changes. If you wear a tweed jacket, you'll probably find that strobing causes an effect that looks like a snake moving around on your shoulders. This can obviously be very distracting for viewers.

Plain clothing works on-screen – unless it's black

The main point to remember is that your appearance should not be more dominant or prominent than what you say. Don't wear memorable clothes unless you're a celebrity or in the fashion industry. Be like the Amish in the Harrison Ford film *Witness*: 'We are plain people.' If you keep your clothes plain, people will remember what you say, not what you wear. If you're a spokesperson on TV or video, plain colours work best. However, it's a good idea to avoid black outfits such as black tops or shirts with black jackets. Black outfits can be difficult to light and look like a solid mass of black with no definition. Black may seem like a safe choice but it does suck in the light and can sometimes make your head look a bit disembodied.

Case study: The 'shirtstorm'

In 2014, Rosetta became the first spacecraft to orbit a comet and, later that year, the first to land a probe on a comet and send back data. This was a significant achievement for the European Space Agency and British astrophysicist Matt Taylor went on TV to celebrate it. Unfortunately for him, his shirt became the story. He was wearing a casual, short-sleeved shirt with scantily clad women forming part of the large pattern. Cue outraged protests on Twitter and condemnation all round for his bad taste and poor judgement, plus the criticism that this illustrated a sexist culture among male scientists. Matt then had to apologise at a press conference – now wearing a plain hoodie – before being able to discuss the historic Rosetta mission (Meikle 2014). The lesson from this is that the clothes you wear on TV do matter. Your best shirt may not always be the best shirt on-screen.

Jacket or no jacket?

Jackets give both men and women instant authority. It's important to remember that a smart jacket, whether part of a suit or not, provides a neat frame in the tight shots used for TV interviews, so always think carefully about whether you should wear a jacket or not.

The two rules for wearing jackets in TV interviews are as follows:

1. **Interviews sitting down**: Always unbutton all of your jacket buttons when sitting down. This prevents the jacket looking untidy by gapping

and sticking out or riding up. If your jacket is long enough, pull it down and sit on the bottom of it to stop it riding up to your ears.
2. **Interviews standing up:** When you're being interviewed standing up or when you're presenting while standing in front of an audience, you should keep your jacket buttoned at least by one button. This makes you look slimmer and smarter. Also, if you're outside standing up, it's usually a lot windier than you think it is when looking out from the comfort of your office. If you keep a button done up, your jacket won't get caught by the wind and flap about. If it's a live interview, you may wonder whether you should grab hold of your jacket. This is a distraction you don't need.

Should you wear a suit?

Whether to wear a suit or not is a matter of individual judgement. In some circumstances, a suit will be appropriate and in others a smart casual look with a jumper or cardigan may work better. A classic suit can confer authority but can also be unmemorable and therefore useful in ensuring that the audience are listening to your messages and not analysing your clothes as well as your content. A jacket and a plain T-shirt top can look smart and even a T-shirt or turtleneck on its own, as pioneered by Mark Zuckerberg and Steve Jobs respectively. But what works for a billionaire may not be as impressive for a middle manager!

Tops with messages

It seems as if there have never been so many messages on clothing. Always remember to ask yourself if having a message on your T-shirt, sweatshirt or hoodie is going to be helpful when you're doing an interview.

Scarves can be hazardous

Scarves can become a hazard in outdoor interviews and blow across your face – and even worse, stick to your lipstick (if you're wearing any). Chunky winter scarves can make your neck look too short and a bit strange. Thinner scarves, even if they're tied in a neat way, can be distracting, as can scarves with large patterns. A plain scarf neatly draped or tied can be useful indoors but don't let it dominate your shot. Always take time to consider whether wearing a scarf is a good idea and can benefit your appearance.

Jewellery and badges

When you're on camera, it's best to avoid jewellery except for plain necklaces. This also applies when presenting on-screen. Statement jewellery can even become the story, as Lady Hale, then head of the UK Supreme Court, found when her large spider brooch received coverage of its own alongside the fact that she was wearing it while reading out a historically significant judgement about the UK's parliament. Always check that you've removed any potentially puzzling items such as badges, brooches, pins or lanyards. You'll have a better impact without them. The only place that people are interviewed on TV wearing lanyards is at conferences where the audience understands the context and everyone is wearing them.

Shirts that work without a tie

If you wear a shirt without a tie, make sure it's a fitted shirt, so that it looks smart. Not all shirts work without ties. However, going tieless doesn't always work if you're a middle-aged man. Not wearing a tie can make you look older, as if you're trying too hard to be on trend or, even worse, as if you're trying to look younger. You're better off sticking with a tie.

When you wear a shirt, always make sure it fits well. Crumpling and creasing are not a good look. For women, a well-fitted shirt will almost always look smarter than a blouse.

Blouses and their many dangers

Until you have to make a presentation or give a TV or video interview, you may never have had to consider the hazards of blouses. However, for public appearances of any kind, blouses bring risks of embarrassment. Why? Because blouse buttons are much more likely to come undone than firmly fixed shirt buttons. And where do blouses come undone? Answer: across the bust, which is always embarrassing. Even if blouses don't come undone, they can look strained and pulled across the bust and create a distraction in the minds of your audience. The straining blouse can dominate the middle of the screen and that's not what you want to happen. Other problems with blouses include fussy patterns and frills and the fact that, unlike shirts, the front seam with the blouse buttons can pull to one side or the other and look very untidy.

My advice is not to wear blouses in any professional setting. Better alternatives are plain shirts with stiff collars, T-shirt-style tops and roll neck or crew neck sweaters. Plain tops with plain necklines partnered with classic jackets are easy to wear and always look smart on-screen and in person. Don't be a fashion victim and wear frills or patterns that are going to confuse your audience. Always choose smart but comfortable clothes and avoid clothes that are too tight or ill fitting.

Skirts and dresses

When you're presenting in person at a meeting or conference, be aware that unless you wear a long skirt or trousers, your knees will be on show to the audience. This also applies to breakfast and daytime TV shows that use sofas for interviews. If you're wearing a dress, be aware of length and the top of the dress. A plain colour and neckline is preferable. Avoid exposed cleavage at all costs. Unless worn under a jacket, large patterns can be dominant and distracting.

Block colours

The late Queen Elizabeth II was well known for wearing block colours. This meant she had numerous outfits with a coat, dress and hat, all in matching colours. When Nicola Sturgeon was the first minister of Scotland, she too made use of block colours, favouring plain dresses with matching jackets. Block colours can convey an image of authority.

Symmetry matters

Humans like symmetry, so asymmetrical clothes don't work well on-screen. If you wear a one-shoulder top or dress, or a top with a stripe or pleat going across it diagonally, your audience will be trying to decode your clothes instead of listening to what you're saying. Most people's faces aren't entirely symmetrical and in everyday life we don't notice this. Interestingly, in the 1980s and 1990s, when Anna Ford was one of the most famous newsreaders in the UK, newspapers were fond of pointing out that, unlike the rest of us mere mortals, her face was almost symmetrical and so worked perfectly for television.

Hair: the long and short of it

You have to take extra care over your hair on-screen because the shots used in TV and video interviews as well as online business meetings always include close-ups. We have nothing else to look at but your face and hair. This means even slight untidiness is exaggerated and can make you look less authoritative than you are in real life. It's important to avoid having hair falling across your face. This isn't just because it will be distracting to the audience but also because you'll feel you'll have to keep moving your hair to one side. Touching your hair on-screen makes you look nervous and unsure of yourself and having to move your hair off your face while you're speaking is never a good look.

 It's easy for long hair to dominate a tight shot on-screen. What wouldn't be noticed so much in normal life can take up a lot of people's attention while watching you. To avoid this, there are steps you can take to prepare yourself. If you have long hair, you can fix it up entirely or partially, so that you pull your hair away from your face. You can also have one side of your hair in front and the other side behind your shoulders. This will stop long hair dominating your image on-screen and distracting your audience. You'll often see this in celebrity stills. Even though this is an asymmetrical style, it can look sleek and elegant. Above all, you should keep long hair away from your face and eyes. People want to see your eyes when you're talking on-screen.

Whatever the length of your hair (presuming you have any), make sure you comb it before any interview or presentation. If you don't, you may look at your recorded interview and find stray bits of hair sticking out or straying across your face. In short, you'll find your hair is letting you down and generally making you look untidy and unprofessional. In TV studios your hair can pick up static electricity and start sticking up without you noticing. To avoid this, if you find yourself in a studio, stroke both your hands over your hair from the top of your head downwards. This will reduce any static by earthing it.

Hairspray is your best friend. Even in a windy outdoor location, it's possible to control your hair. Years of experience as a TV reporter have taught me that it's always windier outside than you think it will be. That's why TV microphones have covers to reduce wind noise. So, if you're interviewed outside, always consider using hairspray.

Body language

People watching you on-screen will be taking in your body language as well as your appearance. They'll pick up whether you're nervous or confident and won't need a qualification in neuro-linguistic programming (NLP) to understand a little of how you're feeling when you're

Why appearance matters

talking. Whether you're presenting or giving an interview, maintaining a calm and confident demeanour plays a large part in getting your audience to listen to you. There are a number of techniques that can help you to achieve this. These include closing your eyes and breathing calmly and deeply five to ten times before you go into the room or the studio where you'll be speaking, as well as preparing thoroughly and ensuring you're on top of your material. It's much easier to be calm and confident when you know what you want to say and how you want to say it. Practising with a trainer like me can help a great deal with your ability to deliver successful presentations and media interviews. If you have a real phobia of public speaking, you may want to consider finding a therapist who can help you overcome your fears.

Your on-screen appearance: a summary

People watching TV interviews are often mentally tidying people on their screens. We're all easily distracted by the images we see. Like the commentators on the British TV programme *Gogglebox*, we do notice people's appearance before we start to listen to them. Our image impression comes first and we have to decode it before we decide to listen. So, it's good practice never to let your hair or clothes be a distraction from what you're saying. Looking smart really pays off and if you do this you'll know that you're doing your best and people aren't silently marking you down as unprofessional and untidy. You don't want your audience to be puzzled or wondering why you're sitting in the dark. There are other obvious no-nos. One of my colleagues was amazed when a woman appeared at an online weekly meeting wearing a dressing gown and a towel around her wet hair. This wasn't just distracting – it was disrespectful to her colleagues. Some of them complained about this and she has now left that employer. Never feel tempted to be that casual, even when meeting colleagues you know well. Here's your checklist for checking your appearance before giving presentations, media interviews or job interviews on-screen.

Your on-screen appearance: a checklist

- Clothes – are they distracting? Check colours, patterns, frills, etc.
- Clothes – are your clothes creased, ill fitting or stained?
- Jewellery and badges – have you removed any puzzling items?
- Make-up – are you wearing any? Is it neatly applied?
- Hair – is it neat and tidy? Is long hair behind your shoulders or fixed up? Can you avoid any hair falling across your face?
- Hair – do you need to use some hairspray?
- Hair – have you brushed your shoulders to remove any stray hairs?
- Jacket – buttoned or unbuttoned?
- Chair – is it comfortable, at a good height for you, without a headrest, and not squeaking?

Chapter 4

Making the most of your presentations

Effective public speaking and the ability to deliver impactful presentations are now vital skills for success in the visual economy, but surveys consistently show that delivering a speech is always high up on the list of many people's top fears, along with fear of spiders, snakes and heights. In fact, a majority of people will admit they're afraid of giving a speech or presentation, even to a small audience of colleagues, let alone to a conference full of strangers. Fears of exposure as a stupid or inadequate and feelings of vulnerability rush in and logical thought flies out the window. The advice in this chapter is designed to prepare you for delivering short or long presentations to colleagues or external audiences and is intended to reduce fears about speaking in public.

Fear of public speaking has a scientific name: glossophobia. This word comes from two Greek words – *glossa*, meaning tongue, and *phobos*, meaning fear or dread. The word reflects the fact that people can literally become tongue tied by fear and panic when standing up in front of an audience. Anxiety about public speaking can have physical effects too. It can mean a person finds it hard to talk because nerves have made their mouth feel dry and, when they do talk, they may shake with nerves, speak too fast and run out of breath. Their mind can go blank and they can't think of anything to say. Later in this chapter, I'll be giving you some advice on how to conquer nerves. But it's important to remember that public speaking doesn't just involve making an impression with your words. Your audience will also be assessing all the visual clues you give them. They'll take in and evaluate your appearance, your image and your body language, as well as any PowerPoint slides you're showing them. If you're giving an external presentation, modern technology means you can easily be filmed and your presentation may have a long life on YouTube or Vimeo.

Members of your audience may also film you and put the video on their own social media. As some businesspeople and politicians have found out to their cost, nowadays there's really no such thing as a private meeting. Comments can be videoed on smartphones, uploaded to social media and be picked up by the mainstream traditional media in minutes. Broadcasting is no longer the sole preserve of broadcasters.

An early example of the visual economy, when everyone started to be able to video and broadcast what well-known people were saying, occurred in 2008 when Chelsea Clinton was talking to students at American colleges and explaining why she supported her mother Hillary as the Democratic Party's senator for New York State. This clip, which was clearly shot on an audience member's phone, is still on YouTube and it is (somewhat ironically) titled 'Chelsea Clinton says why she doesn't talk to the media'. It's a video that perfectly illustrates how the visual economy has changed the world we all live in.

You need to develop speaking skills before you start your first job

When the old text economy was dominant, most education in schools and universities used to be based almost entirely around words. Even when taking practical courses, reading and writing were the main skills that students required to pass examinations, gain qualifications and secure paid employment. Now students are routinely expected to give presentations as part of their studies and they can fail a subject if they don't do this well. There has been some debate in academic institutions about whether it's fair to ask students, some of whom are very nervous about public speaking, to make presentations as part of their coursework. However, many teachers and academics argue that it's good for students to learn how to conquer their fears about speaking in public because practising can help them to decrease these fears and, by gaining experience, they can use this skill in their future careers.

TED talks: the public speaking elephant in the room

'At a time when the right idea presented the right way can ripple across the world at the speed of light... public speaking is the key to unlocking empathy, stirring excitement, sharing knowledge and insights, and promoting a shared dream,' says Chris Anderson (2016), the head of TED, a non-profit organisation that promotes ideas-based talks around the world. The bar for public speaking excellence has been set very high since TED talks started to be posted on the internet in 2006. These talks are all free to view and usually involve one person standing alone on a stage in front of a large audience and talking confidently about their ideas. The talks have become a worldwide phenomenon and have been translated into more than 100 languages. There's also the TED-Ed programme, which offers free educational videos and tools to students and teachers. In 2009, Chris Anderson expanded the organisation with the TEDx initiative. This allows the TED organisation to provide free licences to people who want to host TEDx events in their own area. TEDx stipulates that speakers must appear for free, all events must be non-profit and videos should be released to TED through Commons Media. More than 10,000 of these events have been held, creating an archive of around 100,000 TEDx talks. According to the TED website, these talks are viewed or listened to more than 3 billion times annually.

Case study: The after-lunch graveyard slot

Some years ago, I attended a business conference where I witnessed the worst presentation I've ever seen. Why was it so bad? Well, the speaker started off by apologising for any upcoming mistakes and asking the audience for mercy. He said it was the first time he'd ever delivered a PowerPoint presentation and hoped we would all bear with him if things didn't work. This was a bad start because this was a paid-for conference, so the audience were probably thinking, 'Why am I paying to give my time to someone who isn't being professional?'

Plus, it was a one-day conference, and he had the most difficult slot – the after-lunch graveyard slot. I call it that because in a one-day event, as an audience member, you've done a morning, you've had lunch, you've chatted and socialised and now you have to get back to work and hear about more business stuff, when what you'd actually like to do is have a nap or go home. As a speaker you really have to work at getting the audience back in the room and into work mode. When this particular speaker asked the audience to be kind to him, what he was really saying was that he didn't know what he was doing. I could almost feel the rest of the audience withdrawing and sharpening their teeth for the coming blood sports. We became like Romans pitilessly watching animals and gladiators in bloody combat. And it just got worse and worse. His delivery was poor, halting and apologetic. His slides weren't in the right order and he kept going back and forth to find the right ones. He had too many words on his slides and I can't remember a single thing he said – except that he told some jokes, badly, which the audience didn't find amusing. Tumbleweed definitely rolled through the room several times. When he staggered to a finish, nobody asked any questions, probably because the audience just wanted him to go away.

How to avoid losing your audience

TED talks are a great success story and you can learn a lot by watching and analysing them. You may also find it useful to read Chris Anderson's book, *Ted Talks: The official TED guide to public speaking* (2016). The only problem with TED talks is that they've made a lot of people even more worried about public speaking. How on earth, they wonder, am I going to be as good as a TED speaker? But the key to a successful TED talk isn't complicated. Whether you're presenting to an internal or an external audience, if you want to engage them, the simple truth is that there's no substitute for hard work, planning and preparation. People who deliver TED talks practise and practise and practise. The reason they're so good is because they've put the work in. Some use visual images and some don't but they all look and sound impressive. Based on my many years of giving presentations and advising other people on how best to get their points across, here's my checklist for success so you can do your best and not make any obvious mistakes.

Checklist for effective presentations

Check your travel plans

Even if you've visited a venue before, you should always check your travel plans. Ensure you arrive early, whether you use public transport or a car. If you're presenting at a venue you've never visited before, it's best to research it thoroughly and check travel details at least one day before your presentation.

Check the event seating format

Never assume you'll be sitting or standing. Find out whether you'll be standing at a lectern or sitting on casual chairs with no table in front of you. Or will you face the hazard of sitting high up on a bar stool? Thank goodness I was wearing a trouser suit when that happened to me unexpectedly. I was hosting a panel discussion and, yes, I'd tried to find out what the seating would be in advance, but no one seemed to know until I got there (early) on the evening of the event. You can't always find out what you need to know beforehand. And no, given the choice I wouldn't choose bar stools as there usually isn't a table to put notes on. If you're not using a lectern or there's no table, it's a good idea to take a clipboard or an iPad with your notes. You need something with a hard surface, or you could have papers flapping around and dropping, which is never a smart look.

Research your audience

When you agree to give any presentation it is very important to research your audience. It's vital to know who you'll be talking to. So, before you start doing your preparation, find out who the audience are likely to be and what their interests are. If you're talking at a conference, study the other speakers so that you can avoid any repetition. If you're talking to a group that meets regularly, find out what other speakers they've had, especially those relevant to your topic. When you think about your audience, what sort of questions do you think they might ask you? What do you think this audience wants to know? What added value can you give them? What's the setting and the tone that's required? Do you need slides or not?

Tailor your presentation to your audience

Don't take along a pre-prepared presentation and then, as you're running out of time, say something like 'We'll skip the next three slides because we don't have time'. Or, even worse, 'We'll whizz past these slides because you don't need to know about that.' I expect many of us have seen and heard that sort of thing and it doesn't make the audience feel good. In fact, it's sloppy and it makes people feel that the person talking to them doesn't care about them at all. They've just brought along a standard presentation and not even bothered to edit it to tailor it for the specific audience they're talking to. The absolute worst example of this approach is when the first slide hasn't been altered and has the name and date of a previous event! If you want to look professional, you really don't want to do that ever.

Find out how long you have to speak

It sounds obvious but you should never make an assumption about the length of your slot. Always check with event organisers, the chairs of meetings or committees, or boards of directors. You need to know how long you're expected to speak for and how much time is allowed for questions. You can find out more about handling difficult questions in Chapter 7. When you're speaking at conferences, you often have to be flexible because on the day the organisers may ask you to speak for longer or keep it shorter than your assigned slot because a couple of speakers have overrun or another one has cancelled. The more prepared you are, the more flexible you can be and able to cope with this type of problem.

Keep to your time slot

It's important to count your words and get your timing precise. We've all been to conferences where many of the speakers overrun and lunch or evening drinks are delayed and the audience gets more and more fed up. To avoid being a speaker who runs over, you can use the broadcaster's technique for getting timings right for news reports and bulletins. It's simple. Just count three words per second and you'll get an accurate timing. Divide your total words by 180 to work out the number of minutes you'll be talking. Counting three words a second means that you'll say 180 words in a minute, 360 words in two minutes, 540 words in three minutes and so on.

Prepare your content

Always answer the following questions before you start.

- ✤ Why are you doing this presentation?
- ✤ What do you want to achieve?
- ✤ What are your key messages?
- ✤ What are your visual images?

Having a structure is essential. Plan your presentation with a beginning, middle and end.

Beginning: Don't be timid. It's best to avoid starting off by saying in a monotone something like 'Thank you, Chair, for that kind introduction. Thank you so much for inviting me here today. I'm Jane Soap and I'm head of HR at British Widgets Ltd and we aim to make all your widgets work well. Our company was founded in 1915 and...' Your audience will be drifting off already and you've barely started. It's a better idea to engage the audience and demonstrate your expertise right from the beginning. For example, 'Thank you, Chair. Good morning/afternoon/evening everyone. The issue we're discussing today is one of the most important challenges we're currently facing...' A powerful way to grab the audience's attention is to tell a relevant story. For example, 'Last week/month I was in an office/factory/shop/school/refugee camp and I met a remarkable person/saw something new/unusual first of its kind...' Then introduce yourself *after* the story and deliver your key messages. This technique is often used by people giving TED talks but it's not the only way to structure an effective talk.

For an internal presentation, you'll still need to frame your messages and start off with clear statements. Too many people take refuge in detail, statistics and acronyms without interpreting them properly. However, what your colleagues want to know is what you think the latest facts and figures actually mean. They want you to tell them which figures are important and which are showing negative or positive trends. If you're presenting to a committee or a board, you're in an executive role and will be expected to give an opinion of some kind. For example, 'Thank you, Chair. Good morning/afternoon/evening everyone. As you know, we've been working on changing our x systems for y years and the current situation is improving/showing signs of breakthrough/not yet reaching our targets...'

Always outline what you're going to say, then say it in the middle and explain what you're talking about.

Middle: Use the middle of your presentation to provide support for your key messages at the start. Don't use lots of statistics. A general audience can't take them in and even an audience of fellow experts don't want to see slide after slide of graphs and stats. When presenting to committees and boards, you can provide pre-reads. See advice on this below. If you haven't used an anecdote from real life at the start, make sure you give at least one example in the middle of your presentation. People remember stories about people and are more likely to be convinced by your messages if you include relevant anecdotes that bring your facts and figures to life. However, your anecdotes will need thorough preparation to ensure they're clear, concise and directly relevant to your messages.

End: It's essential to know your ending. The best advice is to memorise it so that if you're talking without notes in the middle of your speech, you always know where you want to get to. If you rehearse and memorise your ending, you'll leave your audience with a convincing and memorable conclusion to your talk, perhaps with a call to action that refers back to your opening theme.

Call to action: What is a call to action? Here are some examples:

- 'So, in conclusion, we need to look at gathering more information on this topic before taking any further steps and should have a further report on this at our next meeting.'
- 'So, as I finish this presentation, I'm asking the committee/board for a decision on proceeding with the strategy I've set out today.'
- 'So, finally, I'm asking the committee/board for a decision on approving the extra budget/transfer of budget to pay for the strategy I've set out today.'

You can also use a call to action with a question. For example:

- 'So, in conclusion, we should all ask ourselves what we can do individually and in our organisations to reduce our climate footprint. Will we be able to say we've reduced our climate impact when we come back for next year's conference?'
- 'So, in conclusion, this is a challenging time for everyone in our field and I've outlined some of the main issues. What practical steps will you be taking to address these challenges?'
- 'So, in conclusion, there is a need to decide whether to go on investing/invest more money in this project and I'd like to ask the committee/board to discuss this and provide a decision.'

Keep it visual and avoid 'death by PowerPoint': It's a sad fact that many people seem to think that the more information they can cram on to their PowerPoint slides, the more expert they will appear to their audience. However, the opposite is the case. The more difficult your slides are to decipher, the more you'll be perceived as a poor communicator. In my experience as a presentation trainer, there seem to be two extremes for presentations. At one end there are people who put far too much information onto their slides, with charts and percentages and graphs that are hard to understand, while at the other end some people seem to have decided it's a good idea to use only images and very little text. Both these approaches can make it hard for audiences to follow the presenter's messages. I've seen a presentation where the speaker's slides featured different wild animals that signified different things, and I confess I got rather lost as to what the zebra meant.

The best use of slides is to have no more than five written points per slide, very simply put, revealing them one after another, with relevant illustrations. The good news is that, once you've simplified your messages into single words or short phrases, you can use AI to tidy up your slides and swiftly make them uniformly well designed. There are many systems available to help you with slide design, including built-in options such as Google Slides and Microsoft PowerPoint. You can download copyright-free images from Canva or Unsplash, try a free trial on Shutterstock, or pay a small amount, usually a monthly subscription, for a bigger choice of images. For presentation templates you can try SlideModel, SlideHunter and SlideGeeks, which offer some free templates and some on subscription. There's a huge choice of resources, so there's no excuse for sticking to complicated charts and graphs. Selecting appropriate images and well-designed templates will not only make your presentations visually appealing but your messages will be more engaging, have more impact and be more memorable for your audience.

Number of slides: It's best to avoid showing a lot of text but it's also a good idea to keep a limit on the number of images you use. Research by Canva in their Visual Economy Report (2023) showed that, after surveying 1,600 business leaders in the US, UK and Australia, the preferred number of PowerPoint slides and report pages is ten. 'Ten pages is the sweet spot for presentation length,' the report states. 'Engagement (views and shares) increases with page count from 1–10 with engagement dropping between 11–30 pages.' Guy Kawasaki, chief evangelist for Canva, recommends this basic outline for your ten slides:

- problem
- your solution
- business model
- underlying magic/technology
- marketing and sales
- competition
- team
- projections and milestones
- status and timeline
- summary and call to action.

He promotes the 10/20/30 rule of PowerPoint. 'It's quite simple,' he says. 'A PowerPoint presentation should have **10 slides**, last no more than **20 minutes**, and contain **no font smaller than 30 points**.' As someone who has trained many people to simplify their PowerPoint presentations, I can confirm that this rule is both practical and useful.

Pre-reads: When you're presenting in a more formal setting to a committee or a board, it's often useful to send out information before the meeting. You can send a full written report or a slide deck. This means that if your slides have to contain complicated graphs and statistics, they can be absorbed by members of the committee or board as pre-reads. Then, when you present to the committee or board, you won't need to use the slides yourself. You can talk clearly and concisely about the content you've already sent out and explain what it means without your audience having to look at complicated images while they're simultaneously trying and failing to keep up with what you're saying. If you have to respond to questions, you can refer to the slides and put them up for discussion if required. What you don't want to do is to confuse people with complicated slides. It's much better to send your pre-reads and then talk without showing any slides.

Props: Don't forget you can use props (also known as visual aids) to illustrate your points. You could bring a product, a book or a report and hold it up while you're talking.

For example: 'The reason we put x on the cover is because she typifies the people we help with our work.' This makes it easy for you to tell a story about a person. This is important because people don't remember lots of statistics – they remember stories about people, so it's a good idea to include these. When I work with NGOs, advising their executives on their presentations to external audiences, it's useful for them to bring products from the projects they're working on to help people climb out of poverty. These can be clothes, jewellery or other products that people in Africa, South America or Asia make for sale. Taking about the value these products have in bringing in money for the communities is highly effective. Showing audiences a new, drought-resistant food crop can also be valuable. Bringing objects that illustrate your message, showing them to people and talking about them can be both powerful and memorable.

Jokes: Unless you're giving an after-dinner speech or a tribute when someone's leaving their job, I'd advise steering clear of jokes. People's sense of humour varies a lot, and you never know who's going to take offence about something you haven't thought of. Also, you have to face the fact that you may not be any good at telling jokes. Even if you do have the skills of an amateur comedian, when you're in a professional setting, can you find appropriate jokes or humorous stories? If a story is considered amusing internally, will it still work externally? Probably not. So, it's best to avoid jokes and the risks they can bring. If you do want to inject a humorous anecdote, try it out on your colleagues first. Never ad-lib on the day. You could inadvertently put your foot into something nasty!

Rehearsal: This is an important part of your preparation for a successful presentation. Always remember the saying 'Failing to prepare means preparing to fail'. Once you've prepared your presentation, it's useful to do run-throughs with a colleague or colleagues to ensure your timing is right and you've included all the key points and necessary details. You can time your presentation and film it so you can see how you're coming across. This means you must schedule time for the preparation of your content and the rehearsal, including using your visual aids and memorising your beginning and ending. Thorough preparation will help you to make a good start. You'll be more confident throughout if you start well. However, you can only do this if you practise your introduction and memorise it. Make sure you know what you're going to say at the start, then you can deliver it calmly and confidently without freezing or hesitating. You can then start to enjoy interacting with your audience. Tailing off and fading away without a strong ending is not an option.

Signposts: You can use some words and phrases as signposts for your audience throughout your presentation. Words such as 'however' and phrases such as 'in contrast' can signal a change of direction to your audience. It's essential to signpost the ending. It's always irritating when a speaker doesn't signal that they're coming to the end of their presentation. Your audience will be waiting for your finale and, if you don't signpost it, you can catch them by surprise. I know that, without a signpost from a speaker, I've often had the reaction, 'Oh I wasn't expecting them to stop. Have they finished? What was that last point?' If you signpost that you're coming to the end, people will perk up and give you even more attention as they prepare to memorise your final point. Ending signposts can be as simple as:

- ✦ and finally…
- ✦ in conclusion…
- ✦ so, to sum up…
- ✦ so, I want to leave you with this thought…

Body language and performance

Movement: Moving around is obviously not a good idea if you're presenting online. If you're presenting in person, you may be videoed, so it's a good idea only to move purposefully, for example, to pick up or put down a prop. Pacing around a stage can feel effective while you're doing it but when you see the recording, you may not be so impressed with yourself. Here are some tips for achieving the most impactful body language.

Feet: Never stand with your feet crossed. This will mean you'll wobble and it looks defensive and underconfident. Also avoid standing with your feet together as if you're a soldier saluting. This makes you raise and tense your shoulders. Always stand with your feet comfortably apart and your shoulders back.

Arms: Don't fold your arms. This restricts your breathing and makes you appear defensive and unsure of yourself.

Hands: Never clench your hands together. Do what the top TV presenters do: with your left hand, hold on to the index and middle fingers of your right hand. Your shoulders will relax and come down and you can hold on as tightly as you like without tensing up. You can also use your hands to illustrate a point when you're presenting in person. If you're presenting on-screen, aim to keep your hands out of shot for most of the time as they may become distracting.

Eyeline: Maintain a steady gaze and look the audience in the eye. Don't hide or look down at your notes. With a larger audience, turn slowly and purposefully to look at different sections of the audience: left, middle, ahead, right, then back to the middle.

Smile: Remember to smile. If you look serious throughout, people may disengage and stop listening. They may also confuse looking serious for looking nervous. If you do come across as nervous, they probably won't find you convincing. Confident people smile. Don't forget to smile during the middle, not just when you begin and end. Everyone's smile is different so it's up to you to work out how you can smile confidently. This doesn't mean grinning with great relief that you've finished! Smiling confidently can mean smiling without showing any teeth but a full smile with teeth works well too. You have to figure out what works for you and makes you look your best.

Sleep: It's essential to get a good night's sleep before an important presentation. Humans don't function at their best if they haven't had sufficient sleep. Staying up and rehearsing into the small hours may not do you any good and may even make you feel worse when you come to make a speech or presentation. Avoid lying in bed staring at the ceiling and going over and over your words.

Nerves: Go into your own zone mentally in the five minutes before you start to talk. Tell yourself that you're calm, well prepared and well equipped to do your best. Take at least five very slow, calming deep breaths. Breathe in and out through your nose and count up to five on each breath in and out. You can practise this as part of your rehearsal and get yourself used to being calm at the start of your presentation. You may still feel a bit nervous but there's nothing wrong with that – it's normal to experience some nerves and, in fact, the adrenaline will make you more alert. What you're aiming for is to make sure you don't feel so overwhelmed by nerves that it will damage your performance. One technique I find useful is changing your mindset. Think of your presentation as a challenge, not a threat.

Performance anxiety: Most people find that if they use the advice and techniques I've outlined in this chapter, they can give a good account of themselves and can become less and less nervous the more practice they have at speaking in public. However, some people find that they need more help than thorough preparation and calming breaths. If you experience serious anxiety and stress when asked to talk to a group, you may wish to consider talking to a doctor about using calming medication or getting help from a therapist.

Voice, pace and tone: A good speech or presentation is never just about content. As the song says: 'It ain't what you do but the way that you do it. That's what gets results.' Remember to vary your pace and tone. Slowing down and using pauses can be very effective. Always speak up but don't speed up. Speeding up means you'll come across as less confident and your talk will be harder to follow and understand. This creates a real danger that people will stop listening to you soon after you've started. If you normally speak fast or you speed up when you're nervous, you should consciously train yourself to speak at a steady pace. Pace yourself in your rehearsals and deliberately speak more slowly than usual. If you speed up, you'll run out of breath and have to stop. If you're not breathing properly, you can make your throat sore and start coughing. Also if you speak too fast you can trip yourself up and stumble over your words. It's a good idea to practise your introduction and the rest of your talk at a slower speed than you normally use until you can deliver it at a steady pace that everyone can follow.

Fake it till you make it: Once you're well prepared, you must tell yourself that you're confident. Make yourself believe that you can deliver an expert presentation. Remember to smile and you'll look and sound more confident – and looking confident will bring you positive results. The more you make yourself look and sound confident, the more you'll believe it yourself, as will your audience. If you tell yourself that your presentation is going to be a disaster, you're likely to find that you've created a self-fulfilling prophecy. Negative thoughts make for a negative performance. Thorough preparation and thinking positively are your best assets. You can't back into the spotlight – you're either there or you're not. Once you've committed to making a presentation, you have the spotlight, so you must prepare well and welcome it. Remember that this isn't a job for perfectionists. You aren't there to make a perfect presentation – you're there to make a good one. And if you can do that, you're doing very well.

What follows is an example of a well-constructed speech that covers a lot of ground and has a clear theme from start to finish. This speech demonstrated to me that you don't have to use images to deliver an effective speech but you do have to look and sound authoritative, have a sound structure and rehearse well. You can watch the video recording on the International Monetary Fund website (see Resources).

Case study: Christine Lagarde

> In 2019, I was lucky enough to witness one of the best speeches I've ever seen. This was a textbook example of how to give a big speech. Not only was the content clear and thought-provoking but the speaker's pace and tone were varied and she commanded the audience with quiet authority right from the start. The event was the annual Tacitus Lecture, hosted by the Worshipful Company of

World Traders at the Guildhall in the City of London, which was packed with an audience of 900 people. The speech was 20 minutes long and was given by the French politician Christine Lagarde, who was then the managing director of the International Monetary Fund (she went on to become president of the European Central Bank). The audience were senior businesspeople, many of them working in the City of London. The title of the speech was 'The Financial Sector: Redefining a Broader Sense of Purpose'. It was a formal setting, so Christine started off with the formalities and then got straight into a story illustrating her theme. She had a clear beginning, middle and end. She covered a lot of ground but kept the audience with her throughout.

Here's the start of her speech, followed by a summary.

'Master, Wardens, Sir David, my Lords, Governor, Aldermen, Sheriff, Chief Commoner, ladies and gentlemen. I am honoured to have been invited to deliver the Tacitus lecture in this magnificent Guildhall. I am also fortunate to be among so many friends, including former colleagues, who know that I have a weakness for good stories. So let me start with a Hollywood story. As you may know, Disney Studios was recently faced with the challenge of creating a sequel to the original *Mary Poppins* movie, which has delighted children and adults for more than half a century. The producers of the new film recreated the magical nanny from P L Travers' books, but they also featured a *new* cast of characters, including a villain who could give everybody a good scare. That villain – yes, you guessed it – is a slick banker who is cheating his way to fortune. In the end, of course, the villain is defeated with a touch of magic.

'So, here is the question: why is the banker the villain? After all, a *healthy* economy requires a *healthy* financial sector that is at the service of people as they pursue better lives for themselves and their children.'

She called this the 'everyday magic' of finance but also pointed out that the caricature of the 'bad banker' has a very long history and this latest version 'seen by millions of children around the world is telling us something about the deeply felt sense of unease about the role of finance in today's world'.

She pointed out that it 'does not take magic' to trace this unease back to the global financial crisis of 2008 and the damage it caused to ordinary people. Then she set out her belief that in too many cases, including with globalisation, the financial sector has 'strayed from its original, noble purpose. And too often, it has worked hard to serve itself rather than serve people and the economy at large. Surely, there must be a better way forward, which brings me to my theme: I believe that we can build a better financial sector, one that is safer, more sustainable and ethically sound. A financial industry with a broader sense of purpose.

'This goal is not just morally just; it's economically right. Why? Because a better financial sector is more important than ever to help deliver on what our 21st century so badly needs: higher employment, greener growth and good living standards for all.'

In the rest of her speech, she outlined how the global financial sector could be improved through better regulation, ethical investments, attention to climate change, more female leadership and other measures. In her conclusion, which she clearly signposted, she referred back to her theme and her story at the start of her talk: 'Let me conclude by returning to Mary Poppins. Remember the scene where the "good banker" teaches his children a lesson about purpose? He argues that they should follow in his footsteps... But the question is whether young people today should consider joining the financial industry. For many of them, the answer comes down to finding a broader sense of purpose, much like Mary Poppins. The genius of her character is that she is serving others with dignity, with a kind heart, with honesty, and with a wicked sense of humour. I think this is a good description of what the financial industry should be all about. Serving others, not yourself – that is the real magic of finance. Thank you.'

Chapter 5

How to appear confident in media interviews

Media interviews are challenging. Whether you're talking online, in a studio or you're indoors or outdoors 'on location', as broadcasters call the real world, you're usually taking on something different from your day-to-day experience. You're walking into a demanding and fast-moving world where you must appear confident and knowledgeable, whatever questions you're asked. And you're speaking on the record. What you say may appear online in social media posts or be quoted by journalists. It's only natural that you may be at the least apprehensive or at worst very worried about giving interviews to journalists in print and on radio, television, video or online. Your stress levels will rise and anxiety may cloud your thoughts. What on earth am I going to say? What if they ask me about x or y or z? The way to cope with this is to sit down calmly and take the time to plan your interview and tackle all those x, y and z issues. This is the only way to ensure success. You don't want to look worried during media interviews.

Many radio interviews are no longer simply audio

but are now livestreamed, so your image matters. This has caught out a number of male TV reporters and newsreaders across the world who have been seen broadcasting while wearing a jacket and shirt but only boxer shorts. It's also important to note that sitting in front of a mirror is never a good idea when you're online, as the next case study illustrates.

Case study: The mayor of Antwerp

> Antwerp is the second largest city in Belgium and very important to the Belgian economy. Even so, interviews with the mayor of Antwerp don't usually gain much attention outside Belgium. However, when he was giving an interview to a Flemish language radio station at the beginning of 2021, Mayor Bart de Wever attracted a lot of comment because he spoke on the radio from his home while sitting in front of a large mirror that revealed his bare legs and boxer shorts. There were comments on social media during the interview so, after a few minutes, the interviewer had to ask him about his clothes. She said: 'I'm a little distracted, Bart de Wever. You are wearing a very nice shirt; probably you wore it especially for us because you know people are watching on the Radio 2 app. But under that shirt, could it be that you are there in your underwear?' The mayor replied, 'How do you know that?' Realising his mistake, he said, 'I'm probably sitting in front of a mirror. I had not taken that into account. The year begins with a particularly embarrassing moment. I'll remember this for a long time.'

All this was reported online and in newspapers in the UK, with helpful subtitles from Flemish to English (Newman 2021).

Other visual mistakes

When you're giving TV or radio interviews in studios, there are skilled technicians who'll ensure that you look and sound professional. When you're broadcasting online from your home or office, you have to make sure that you don't make mistakes with lighting and framing your shot. For example, broadcasters may ask you to use a landscape shot as they don't want a portrait shot coming up on the screen that their interviewer is talking to. They want you to be framed in a landscape shot. So, it's best practice not to use your phone for a TV interview unless you're a witness to a breaking news story. In that case broadcasters are grateful for any eyewitness accounts they can get and the more rough and ready the content the better as it adds to the drama of the news story. Advice on getting your framing and lighting right is in Chapter 3. This chapter gives you advice on how to prepare your content and make sure you don't appear foolish and inexpert during your interviews.

In broadcasting, everyone's an expert

Many people who have joined my media training courses arrive after having done one or two broadcast interviews without training. This experience swiftly makes them realise that they've been on a high wire without a safety net and they do need help to be able to construct their safety net and balance themselves on the high wire with confidence. They report being startled when an interviewer introduces them as an expert. Interviewers blithely say, 'And we're joined now by Jane Soap, who is an expert on this topic' – not realising the terror they're striking into the hearts of their interviewees, who are broadcasting rookies.

Understand the deal

As an interviewee, you may think that you're not an expert. 'Lots of people know more than I do,' people tell me when attending my media training courses. However, there's an unspoken deal going on whenever you're on the radio or TV. The deal is that you don't actually have to be the world's greatest expert, but you do have to know more than the audience does about your area of expertise. Otherwise, why are *you* on the radio or TV instead of them? You've been given the precious opportunity to broadcast to a large number of people because you know more than the audience – and the interviewer – about the topic you're talking about. This is what the interviewer and the audience expect.

What does your audience want?

Let's look at the audience for your broadcast interviews. Who are they? It's important to realise that, when it comes to radio and TV stations and their programmes, most people now have the widest choice of content they've ever had. However, when you're on a TV or radio news programme, your audience have chosen to watch or listen to news and current affairs content in the face of thousands of other content opportunities all available at the same time. So, what does this mean for you? It means that the audience you're talking to are really interested in news and current affairs and are therefore well informed. And they want to know more.

Getting the best results from media interviews

If you share some interesting, new information, the audience might talk about your interview with their colleagues, family and friends, look up your organisation online, read content on your website and start following you on social media. They might post something positive about you and your work or even start to do business with you, buy your products or services, visit your exhibition, read your book or report, or donate to your cause. These are the excellent results you should be aiming for every time.

Looking confident and talking fluently are crucial in broadcasting

It's obviously no use to broadcasters to book a top expert for an interview if they're nervous or hesitant or can't talk clearly and succinctly about their topic to a general audience. Shy, introverted scientists and academics devoted to their own technical language don't succeed in broadcast news interviews. I clearly remember noticing this when I moved from print journalism to working as a reporter for the BBC and saying to some friends still working in print journalism that broadcast journalism is very different from print, not only in terms of the medium itself but also in terms of content from experts. In print, a journalist can write up quotes in a different order and help them communicate their ideas to the readers. In broadcasting, most interviewees are live on air. This means you alone are responsible for getting your messages across in a good order for maximum impact so that the audience will remember them and stick with you for the whole interview. This makes planning your messages essential. Failing to prepare is the enemy of fluency. It's also the enemy of confidence. Preparation builds up your confidence. Lack of preparation can lead to unnecessary panic and hesitancy and make you look a bit stupid instead of the expert that you are.

What's your interview agenda?

When you give an interview to broadcasters, your task is to prepare the agenda for your interview. In every interview, there's always a battle for the agenda. You and the interviewer may have the same agenda but you may have different ones. If, as an interviewee, you don't have an agenda, you'll find it hard to succeed in getting anything positive across to the public because you'll just answer the questions put to you. This runs the risk that the interviewer will get you talking about something that's not on your agenda and you won't get across what you want to say.

Don't let aggressive political interviews worry you

The fact that political interviews are tougher and more aggressive than general news and business interviews can give people a distorted view that most media interviews are in 'attack' mode. This won't be the case for the majority of general news interviews. Many people also worry that, even if they're not being attacked during an interview, they'll face questions to which they don't know the answers and they'll end up looking stupid. This is a normal response but there are ways to cope with all the questions you could be asked, and you'll find these in the next chapter.

How to get your eyeline right for TV and video

A TV producer once said to me, 'Eyeline is everything on TV. If a speaker gets their eyeline wrong, we just won't listen to them.' There are only two eyelines for TV interviews – look at the interviewer or look at the camera. If you don't follow these rules, you'll look odd, the audience will notice and at the very least will consider you to be unprofessional. Getting your eyeline right is essential to looking confident on TV and video. How do you know which eyeline to choose? Always ask the interviewer, a nearby researcher or the camera operator if there is one. Always check – never assume you know where to look.

Eyeline one: look at the interviewer

When you're being interviewed in person, either in a studio or on location, you should look at the interviewer. If you're being interviewed by a TV reporter or presenter, you must avoid looking at the camera. This is not normal or natural but you have to train yourself to do it. To maintain eye contact throughout a face-to-face interview, you can look at the point on the interviewer's face between their eyebrows. This will enable you to keep a steady eyeline without feeling rude or odd by staring at them.

Eyeline two: look at the camera

When you're giving remote interviews from a studio or outdoors via a link or online, you should look at the camera throughout your interview. This type of interview is called a remote interview because you're remote from the studio from which the programme is being transmitted. Remote interviews are also called 'down the line' interviews. This is because when TV presenters are interviewing you in a studio separate from theirs, they have to book lines to link up their studio with the remote studio or use a satellite link to link up with a reporter on location, which simply means an interview not being conducted in a studio. In order to look convincing to the audience during remote interviews, you must talk to the camera throughout your interview. This applies whether you're sitting or standing. To do this convincingly you do need to practise, and media training will help with this.

You must take time to prepare for media interviews

When you agree to give a media interview, you should treat it as the most important three or four minutes of your life so far and take time to prepare. How much time? For any interview, it's advisable to prepare for a minimum of at least one hour. If you don't have any or much experience of giving broadcast interviews, two hours is better. Why so long for such a short interview? Because it definitely isn't enough just to discuss your headline points with colleagues for a few minutes and then expect to be able to talk expertly and professionally in an interview. It's essential to check all your facts and figures or you'll find that you don't have sufficient knowledge to answer the interviewer's questions clearly and concisely in a high-pressure environment. If you haven't done this type of preparation before, you'll be surprised by how much time you do need to check up on your data, headline phrases and supporting points. Ask your colleagues, 'We always say that but where did we get those figures from?' One of the worst feelings during a media interview is to realise that you want to use a phrase, a fact or a figure but you haven't checked it out so you're not absolutely sure you can use it 'on the record' in a broadcast interview. If you don't prepare, even for a friendly and positive interview, *every* question, even positive ones, will seem like a threat and you'll come across as hesitant and unsure.

Giving effective media interviews is a lot harder than it looks

Why is this? It's because the media exists in its own world with its own rules. We all absorb these rules as listeners or viewers. But, just as going to the theatre doesn't mean you can write a play, it's also true that hearing or watching a lot of news doesn't mean you know how to deliver an effective TV interview. Many people who have come to me for media training are in the position of having done a couple of interviews where some things went right and a few things went wrong, and they realise they will be wise to get media training in order to avoid things going wrong in future. Others realise it's sensible to get media training to find out how to plan and deliver their media interviews before taking on any interviews at all.

Common questions about media interviews

- How can I avoid looking and sounding stupid?
- What do I do if I can't answer the questions?
- What do I do if my mind goes blank?
- Can I see the questions before the interview?
- Can they ask me anything?
- Is the reporter out to get me?
- How do I stop myself speeding up and talking too much when I'm nervous?
- I've done a couple of bad interviews before – how can I stop worrying and do better?

Here are the answers:

How can I avoid looking and sounding stupid?

The best ways to avoid this are to get your eyeline right, be on top of your messages and thoroughly prepare for your interview, both in terms of your content and your appearance. (See Chapters 3 and 4 for advice on looking professional online.) It is also very important when you are in a studio or with a broadcast crew never to say or do anything that you don't want to be broadcast.

Case study: Sainsbury's boss forgets the basics

You're never too big to be reminded of the basics. Astonished TV news viewers saw Mike Coupe, then the boss of Sainsbury's, Britain's second-largest supermarket chain, happily singing 'We're in the money. The sky is sunny, let's lend it, spend it, send it rolling along' while in a TV studio waiting to be interviewed about a proposed merger of Sainsbury's and Asda in April 2018. No matter how many TV interviews you've done – no matter that you're a top boss and becoming even more so as the intended head of the proposed largest supermarket business in the UK, my media training advice is always the same. Never forget about the microphones and cameras. Don't say or do anything in a TV studio that you don't want to be broadcast. It really is Media Interviews 101.

News reporters were pinching themselves that they were so lucky. Not only did a mega boss look a bit silly by singing a song, but also, in what appeared to be a big Freudian slip-up – the words were just so deliciously appropriate for one of the UK's biggest ever business stories. From Mr Coupe's point of view, it was bad enough to be seen to be singing anything at all. But to pick that particular song clinched his fate. There was no way the news bulletins were not going to pick up on what he called 'an unguarded moment trying to compose myself before a TV interview' during a possible £12bn deal. Later the same day he solemnly apologised in case he had given offence. He said: 'It was an unfortunate choice of song, from the musical 42nd Street, which I saw last year, and I apologise if I have offended anyone.' (BBC News 2018)

But his apology rather misses the point. What Mr Coupe's 'unguarded moment' did was to make him look a bit stupid and possibly also greedy and generally to undermine and trivialise discussion of a very serious day for Sainsbury's and Asda and their more than 330,000 employees. It broke the spell of authority which TV interviews are supposed to provide and made him the subject of ridicule in traditional media and across social media. The merger deal eventually did not go ahead but, in media terms, what should have been a positive day for Sainsbury's and Asda when announcing their proposed merger was overshadowed by negative headlines about his singing. In addition, the story lives on as numerous later articles about him also refer to this rather embarrassing incident.

What shall I do if I can't answer the questions?

When you're preparing for your interviews, don't focus on the questions more than the answers. Of course, it's important to write down a list of all the questions you think that the interviewer might ask you. But you shouldn't get hung up on questions. Your job is to make statements that positively promote your company/organisation/event/book/report, etc. Your job is to provide some interesting facts, figures and stories that illustrate how what you're talking about works in real life. No matter what the interviewers may want you to think, your answers will be more interesting to the public than most of their questions.

It doesn't matter if you don't get all the interviewer's questions in advance. What's important is to get an idea of which areas the interviewer wants to cover. What do they want to include in the interview? Then you can make sure you can cover those areas and say interesting things about those topics as well as get your own agenda across. For advice about answering tricky questions, read the next chapter.

What do I do if my mind goes blank?

It's not uncommon for people who aren't used to broadcasting to find that they have a blank moment during a TV or radio interview when they don't know what to say. To cope with this, it's essential to be able to move to one of your prepared messages. If your mind goes blank once you've given part of your statement, the best course of action is to stop talking. It's the interviewer's job to keep the show on the road and drive the interview forward. If you stop talking, they'll ask you something else. The most important thing to remember is that you're far less likely to have a 'rabbit in the headlights' moment if you prepare thoroughly and practise answering questions. This will mean that your mind and your mouth are on top of your content and you have phrases ready to use that you've practised saying. Even if you're asked a totally unexpected question, you'll be able to move confidently to what you want to say.

Case study: Two tough interviewees

In their heyday, former British prime minister Margaret Thatcher and former US secretary of state Henry Kissinger concentrated more on their answers than the questions. Margaret Thatcher was said to have put down papers in front of her interviewers and declare, 'There are my answers. What are your questions?' Similarly, Henry Kissinger's approach was reported to be, 'Who's got questions for my answers?' These two are legendary political figures of the 20th century, so I'm not suggesting you follow their example. It's not a good idea for you to take this approach to your media interviews. However, you don't have to be in the big league to realise it's a good idea to spend time preparing solid, interesting statements for your media interviews.

Can I see the questions before the interview?

You can ask for and sometimes be given questions that journalists want to ask you about your topic. However, even if you do get some questions in advance, the journalist will ask you more than that. As an interviewer myself, I know that a new question can occur to me during an interview. A good media interviewer doesn't stick to a list of pre-prepared questions. If you say something interesting that they haven't heard before, they'll ask you a question about that. And if their questions do go off on a different track that you've introduced into the interview, that should be good news for you because they'll be asking you to talk about what's on your agenda. It will only be bad news if you say something unplanned and the interviewer finds it really interesting and you find yourself being taken away from your key messages. This is easily done if you're not properly prepared and you haven't fully thought through what you want to say.

Can they ask me anything?

Yes, they can. This is an uncomfortable truth that you just have to accept. But this doesn't mean you can't handle it. In Chapter 7, you'll find detailed advice on handling difficult questions.

How do I stop myself speeding up when I'm nervous?

It's quite common for people to talk faster when they're nervous. Some people will do this throughout an interview. In my experience as a media trainer, most people who speed up will do this at the start of their interview and then, as they gain more confidence, their pace will settle down. It's a disservice to your audience if you speak so fast that people have to strain to concentrate on what you're saying. The best way to conquer this is first to be aware that you're speeding up; and second, to practise pacing yourself and deliberately slowing down your delivery. There's a small minority of people who react in the opposite way and speak slowly and quietly when they're under pressure. This is also a disadvantage for media interviews and, if this affects you, you can train yourself to raise your volume and pace whenever you're broadcasting. The more practical experience you get delivering presentations or media interviews, the more you'll be able to conquer your nerves and improve your pace of delivery.

How do I stop myself talking too much when I'm nervous?

The first step to ensuring that you don't talk too much is recognising that you're doing this. The next step is training yourself to stop talking. Practise keeping your points short. Media interviews are often only a few minutes long. You don't need to make long statements. Russian President Vladimir Putin demonstrated how this doesn't work when, in his much-publicised interview with the American broadcaster Tucker Carlson, he spoke for more than half an hour when giving his first answer (Rainsford 2024). This was an extraordinary interview and I don't recommend it as a template to follow for either an interviewee or an interviewer.

To get the feel of what normally works in TV interviews, it's useful to record some news programmes and time the length of the interviews and the statements people make. When you're preparing for a media interview, you can time yourself on the stopwatch on your phone. You can work out how to keep your statements to around 30 or 40 seconds. Counting your words as broadcasters do, at three words per second, that's 90 to 120 words. Once you've done this preparation, when you've made your points during your interview, you can stop and wait for the next question.

I've done a couple of bad interviews – how can I stop worrying and do better?

Giving media interviews is not a job for a perfectionist. If you want to do a perfect interview, you'll always be disappointed. I can't count the number of times where, during a media training session, one person will say that they've just done a terrible interview, but when it's played back to the group, everyone else disagrees and says they didn't even notice that the person had hesitated or stumbled when answering some questions. When they're nervous, people go into 'road traffic accident' mode, with their brain going into slow motion, and they think that a slight hesitation has taken two or three seconds when in fact it was only half a second. Blink and you'll miss it. So sometimes your terrible interview is not as bad as you think.

Giving a media interview is not like talking about a topic internally

When you're broadcasting, anyone can pick you up on what you say. Thanks to social media, you can gain more publicity for your interviews than simply relying on traditional media. But you have to be sure you're not going to be called out for making mistakes or being controversial in ways that could be damaging to your reputation and your organisation's reputation. You might think 'Well, we always say that about this issue', but it might turn out to be inaccurate, unproveable or simply not the right thing to say externally. It might be appropriate as an internal comment but not in a broadcast interview when it becomes open to much more scrutiny. You must be sure about all of your statements.

Case study: Don't write notes on your hands

Preparation enables you to be fluent and confident without needing to rely on notes. While you can have notes with you for a radio interview, it's best to have just one sheet of paper with a few bullet points listing key facts and figures that you must include in your interview. You won't have time to look through a report or news release to find the information you require. In my experience, most people don't look at their notes during their radio interviews, but they're reassured by the 'comfort blanket' of having the notes with them. For radio interviews, you can have notes and glance at them, but you can't have any notes in TV interviews. You're expected to speak without them. Don't try to get around this by writing notes on your hands. Clients have often asked me about using this technique and some have tried it during their media training interviews. I strongly advise against this because it doesn't work.

It most definitely didn't work for British MP Greg Hands. When he was chairman of the Conservative Party, he gave some interviews to TV news programmes seeking to boost Conservative votes before important local council elections. However, the media didn't bother reporting his political messages. They just reported that Greg Hands had lived up to his surname by writing what appeared to be notes in ink on the palms of his hands (Tapsfield 2023). They pointed out that the writing was clearly visible and the ink was smudged, probably because his palms were moist due to nerves and sweating

> under the studio lights. As I've pointed out to clients, and as Greg Hands discovered, sweat will smudge notes on your hands and render them useless. In addition, you run the risk of looking ridiculous and losing the respect of the audience.

Questions to ask before media interviews

Not all media interviews are the same. Here are the practical interview planning tips that we give our clients and they find really useful. The guiding principles to follow are: never assume anything and always ask questions before your interviews.

Are you the right person to do this interview or should it be a colleague?

Discuss with the researcher or producer how they want to tackle your topic. Is the angle they're taking one that suits you? Never let yourself be rushed into doing an interview.

If you decide to do the interview, what type of media interview(s) are you being asked to give?

For example, how long is the interview expected to be? Is the interview live or recorded?

Is it in a studio with an interviewer or in a remote/separate studio, or online? Will you be outdoors standing up, or indoors (not in a studio) sitting or standing? You need to know what to expect. You don't want to be surprised and flustered by finding yourself alone in a studio talking to a camera when you had assumed you'd be talking to a presenter, or standing up outside when you'd assumed you'd be sitting in your office, or vice versa.

Will other people be interviewed about my topic?

Will you be on your own or will you be expected to take part in a discussion? Establish how many people will be involved and, if possible, who they are. Sometimes broadcasters don't have all the people booked in for the discussion when they talk to you, but it's important for you to have as much information as possible so you know what other people, who will almost always have opposing views to yours, will be saying. Alternatively, will another expert be interviewed before or after you? What do you think these people will say? How will you deal with their claims if they disagree with you? The key point about being involved in a discussion is that you'll have less time to make your points. If you don't go first, an interviewer will typically turn to you and ask 'What do you make of that?' The biggest mistake you can make is to use your time to carefully demolish your opponent's points and not get to your own agenda. It's always best to say something like 'Well, we don't agree with that. We think a better way of tackling this problem is...' And move quickly to making your own points.

Interview content: what do I want to talk about?

What do the broadcasters say they want you to talk about? How can you make sure that when you talk about this topic you're promoting your own expertise? Can you suggest interesting topics that *you* want to talk about and they haven't thought of? If you say something interesting about your topic, they may decide to go with your angle and make your life a lot easier.

What's in the news that I might be asked about?

What other possible interview content, the wider context or relevant current issues could you be asked about? Always ask yourself, what's in the news about my field at the moment? Interviewers may ask you about anything in the news that they think is relevant to your expertise. What will you be prepared to comment on? How will you state that you can't/don't choose to comment? Do an online search or ask colleagues for help with this.

Practical planning: travel

Always be prepared. Plan your travel to the interview venue and make sure you have the exact address and the entrance you need to go to. Some broadcasting venues have more than one entrance. You don't want to lose five minutes while you rush to the other end of the building. If it's a national programme, ask if they can send a car to take you to the studio. Always ask for a contact name and mobile number for a researcher or producer on the programme.

Practical planning: online interviews

If your interview is online, check that your space at work or home is suitable for media interviews. See Chapter 3 for advice on lighting, backgrounds, framing, etc.

Practical planning: appearance and grooming

Plan what you're going to wear for your interview and make sure it's suitable for on-screen appearances. See Chapter 4 for detailed advice on this. Always comb or brush your hair and ensure it's tidy before you go into a studio or switch on your camera to check.

How can I plan to be early?

Always be early for your media interviews. Broadcasting is very time sensitive and if you're even a minute late, whether in person or online, you may miss your slot and an important chance to promote your work. Being early also gives you time to compose yourself and be ready for the start of your interview. You'll never do well if you arrive late and flustered. Being early also gives you time to go to the bathroom and ensure you don't get that 'I wish I'd gone to the loo' feeling that nerves can bring on just before your interview, which will make it even more of an ordeal.

Case study: They came to me ten minutes early

> Whenever I do media interviews myself, I do, of course, take my own advice. I commit time to prepare thoroughly and work out my headline messages plus supporting facts and figures and real-life examples. I work on handling any tricky topics and make sure I'm ready early. This advice stood me in good stead when I did an interview with the UK broadcaster Talk TV late on a Sunday evening. And that's another important

thing to note about media interviews – they often don't take place during normal working hours. You may be asked to give interviews early in the morning, or late at night and at the weekend as well as during 'office hours'. You have to make the effort to fit in with the media and, if you're not prepared to do that, you should give up on the idea of doing a lot of media interviews. When my interview was booked, I was told the Talk TV presenter would come to me by 11.30 pm and the good news was that I didn't have to go to their studio. So, I was at home on my laptop, and had taken my own advice on framing, background, lighting, etc, and was ready by 11.15 pm. This turned out to be a good idea as, just after 11.15 pm, the producer unexpectedly told me that they wanted to start my interview at 11.20 pm, which they did. TV broadcasting is not an exact science, to say the least.

Your broadcast interview plan

Before:

- ✦ Write down your three main points as bullet points. This will help you to practise talking around them so that you won't sound over-rehearsed.
- ✦ Decide on the wording you'll use to support your headline points.
- ✦ Select some facts and figures that will drive home your points and check them all.
- ✦ Select some real-life examples that illustrate what you're talking about.
- ✦ Prepare for negative questions. See the next chapter for detailed advice about how to handle these.
- ✦ Do a practice interview with a colleague.

After:

- ✦ Always record your interviews and watch or listen back to them. You need to know what worked and what didn't. Do you look positive or nervous? Should you smile more or smile less? If you watch your interviews, you can build on your strengths and work on your weaknesses. If you don't take the time to analyse your interviews, you'll never improve or learn how to give your best performance.
- ✦ Promote your interviews on your website and in your mailings.
- ✦ Promote your interviews on social media.
- ✦ Take on board any useful comments on social media.
- ✦ Don't get involved in any 'fights' on social media.

And finally...

If you follow the advice in this chapter, you'll have a good chance of looking credible when you take on broadcast media interviews. However, you'll do even better if you book some media training sessions and practise your interviews with me and my colleagues at TV News London. We can enable you to look and sound your best whenever you take on a media interview. Clients often tell me that, before they had media training, they were very worried about every media interview and the threat of stumbling or coming to a halt, and generally looking stupid. After their media training they understand what they need to do to prepare and deliver effective interviews and they can view the whole experience as a challenge but no longer a threat.

Chapter 6

How to handle difficult questions

This chapter will give you the techniques for looking and sounding confident and authoritative when coping with challenging, hostile or unexpected questions, whether you're giving a media interview, taking part in a conference discussion or answering questions after a presentation or in a meeting. You need to think about obvious negative questions and work out your best approach to handling them before you go into a meeting, make a presentation or face a media interview. However, it's impossible to prepare an exact answer to every question you might be asked. What you can do is to prepare what you want to say and then swiftly get to your points using the techniques outlined in this chapter. Whatever questions you're asked, it's important to learn how to retain your composure and authority. Frowning deeply or appearing to be a startled goldfish are never good looks. Train yourself to think on your feet and get to the points you want to make as smoothly as possible.

To pivot or not to pivot…

Every November since 2002, the UK version of the globally successful reality show *I'm a Celebrity… Get Me Out Of Here* has launched its knockout competition to find out which of the famous people taking part can take on tough challenges, including eating insects and unmentionable parts of animals, and be crowned as King or Queen of the Jungle. When former British secretary of state for health and social care Matt Hancock took part in 2022 and came third, one of the things he talked about was media interviews and how politicians are trained to cope with tricky questions. He said, 'In politics, it's called the pivot. And so you have to give enough of a link to the question that it doesn't look like you're avoiding the question while pivoting, and a good pivot is admirable.' Some of his campmates and the journalists writing about this 'revelation' described the pivot as a technique for politicians who want to dodge questions (Jefferies 2022). However, it can be a useful technique for making sure you get across your key messages. The pivot using the word 'look' was a favourite tool of former British prime minister Tony Blair. He would often say in the middle of an interview something like 'Look, the real issue here is…' or simply, 'Look' – then he would carry on making the points he wanted to make.

Bridging is less obvious and can be more effective

People often complain that politicians don't answer questions in media interviews and in my opinion using the pivot doesn't help with this problem. The pivot is more abrupt than the more subtle technique of making a bridge. Saying 'Look' or 'Well, the main point here is...' makes it much more obvious to the audience that you're changing the subject than if you use a bridge. If you're not a politician, your interviews won't be as tough and you can change the subject without being ruthlessly pursued by the interviewer, and what's more, most of your audience won't notice this. You can be ready to sidestep irrelevant, tricky, hostile, difficult and unexpected questions by using the bridging technique, which I explain below.

The answer to all these fears and worries about tricky questions is to recognise that you can't prepare an answer to every question. You just have to accept this. There's no way you can think of absolutely everything an interviewer could ask you. However, you can prepare for obvious questions about your area of expertise, the wider field that you work in and current news topics that an interviewer could relate to your field. As well as accepting that you can't expect to answer every question directly, you should remind yourself that you're not at school or university. An interview is not an exam, and you don't have to answer every question in the exact terms it's put to you. What you must do, however, is address the questions and not ignore them entirely. This technique is used every day by people giving interviews on radio and TV. I guarantee that once I've explained bridging you'll start spotting people doing it all the time.

What is bridging and how does it work?

Bridging is an essential technique for getting your messages across in media interviews and meetings. It's called bridging because you make a bridge away from a question you don't want to answer, or a question you don't have an answer for. You do this by bridging across to your own messages. Bridging is easily remembered using the acronym ABC. This stands for 'address, bridge, communicate'. Your task is to get from A to C via B.

What does this formula do? In simple terms, it helps you to change the subject and talk about something you do know about. Bridging enables you to move away from a tricky or unexpected question and get your messages across, leaving any nasty question far behind and forgotten. It also enables you to fill up your time with getting across your point of view and avoiding a succession of negative questions that may not give a positive impression of you and your organisation.

It's important to understand that bridging isn't about ignoring questions. You should always address a question – briefly – and then move to your own messages. If you ignore a question, your interviewer or a questioner after your presentation will have the opportunity to point out that you haven't answered the question and then ask you a tricky question again. This makes you seem defensive and pushes you into a corner where you may get trapped into saying something you don't want to.

You know you've succeeded with bridging when, having bridged in a media interview, your interviewer then moves on to ask you about what you've just said, or your questioner in a meeting doesn't repeat the tricky

How to handle difficult questions

question you've just bridged away from. The chair then moves on to the next question from someone else. If you use the bridging techniques confidently and naturally you'll sound positive rather than evasive.

Here are three examples of interview bridges:

1. What I can tell you is...

- Well, I don't have information about that, but what I can tell you is...
- We haven't looked specifically at that, but what I can tell you is...
- Well, that's an interesting figure/fact that I'm not familiar with, but what I can tell you is...
- I don't have the figures for ten years ago but what I can tell you is that five years ago...
- I don't think anyone in our industry has figures for that but what I can tell you is that...

2. Yes, but...

- Yes, that's a very important issue, but we think the central issue here is...
- Yes, that is important, but what's even more important is...
- Yes, that's what our recent survey showed, but it also revealed that people think...
- Yes, I know that's what a lot of people think, but that isn't correct/isn't the whole story – what's actually happening is...
- Well, that's what people used to think, but the latest information/research shows...

3. The rebuttal

It's essential to rebut questions that are incorrect or ill informed. If you don't point out something incorrect, it will confuse the audience, who'll assume that the interviewer is correct unless you tell them otherwise and give them the correct information. If they hear the interviewer say something wrong, they may pause and think to themselves something like 'Well, I didn't think that was right, but they haven't said it's wrong so it must be right.' Or they may simply think you're not as well informed as you'd seemed. This means you run the risk of losing the audience's attention and you may not get it back.

Examples of rebuttal:

- No, that's not the case – what's actually happening is...
- No, that's not correct – the latest information/research shows...
- No, if I could correct you on that – the latest information we have shows the numbers are actually...
- Before I answer that, it's important to note that the figure/date you've just given is incorrect. The correct figure/date is...

Successful bridging requires preparation

You can only use bridging successfully if you have somewhere to bridge to. If you don't have your messages prepared, then you won't have anywhere safe to go. A bridge to nowhere is no use at all. If you stop talking after giving a very short answer, the interviewer can just go back and ask you the same questions again. Once you've made your bridge and crossed over it, you should always continue talking and getting your positive messages across so that you leave any tricky/nasty/negative questions far behind you.

How do I stop being afraid of the next question?

As well as suffering from nerves, another reason why some people give answers that go on for too long is because they're afraid of the next question. They think that if they keep talking this will somehow keep them safe and protected from the dreaded next question. However, most people who watch TV and radio news will know when someone's talking too much and they'll get bored and lose respect for you. They may even switch to another broadcaster and you definitely don't want that to happen. So, it's really worth making sure your statements aren't too long for broadcasting. Similarly, if you keep talking for too long when answering questions at a meeting, you run the risk of losing your audience's attention. When you stop talking and get another question you should swiftly work out what the core of the question is and address it. If it's on your agenda, you can talk about it – but if it's not on your agenda, you're ready to make a bridge away from it to go where you want to. Learning the bridging technique will help you to conquer your fears about the next question and become a confident spokesperson.

There will always be more questions than answers

There's a famous song by the late, great singer Johnny Nash entitled 'There Are More Questions Than Answers', and this is a useful phrase to remember when you're preparing for a media interview. You have to accept that there will always be more questions than answers. But if you concentrate on preparing and delivering what *you* want to say, and then use bridging, you can make your answers fit numerous questions.

Case study: The space scientist

A few years back, the BBC radio presenter John Humphrys was interviewing a space scientist on Radio 4's *Today* programme. The scientist was talking about the pros and cons of sending manned and unmanned vessels into space. He started off well. He kept going very well. He explained clearly how much more cost effective it was not to send people but just to send unmanned machines that could go further out into space and find out much more than astronauts could. He was fluent and informative and he managed to get a lot of good stuff across without interruption, but then Humphrys suddenly seemed to wake up and asked, 'That star you just mentioned – how far away is it?' There was a slight pause. The scientist was obviously a bit rattled but tried to get away from the question by talking about something else. However, Humphrys, a renowned 'attack dog' interviewer, was clearly scenting blood and wouldn't be deflected. 'Yes, but that star you just mentioned,' he said again – and then uttered the killer statement, 'I think the public needs to know how far away it is.' This caused the interviewee to collapse. He confessed he didn't know how far away the star was and came to a crashing halt. Oh dear. This was such a shame and it shouldn't have

How to handle difficult questions

happened. In fact, this collapse of the scientist's credibility was easily avoidable.

There are a number of things he could have done better. First: never mention a place that you don't have some facts and figures about. Second: you must be prepared for follow-up questions about anything you've mentioned. Remember that you don't have to know everything; you just have to show that you know more than your interviewer and your audience, which, let's face it, isn't hard when dealing with astronomy. He could have bridged and thought on his feet. He could have said, 'Well, I don't have the exact figure to hand, but NASA astronomers calculate that it takes an average of six years to reach Jupiter from Earth and this star system is far beyond that, so it really is a very long way away.' And then he could've just kept on talking about space science and the need for unmanned space vehicles. What he failed to take into account was the fact that, statistically, a majority of the *Today* programme's audience are not scientists. In fact, I'll bet that a majority of listeners are, like me, unable to answer a simple question about how far away Jupiter is or how big a light year is. What the audience does know is that it's an awfully big distance. So, if the space scientist had talked about light years and big numbers, we would all have been impressed and continued thinking of him as an expert – and not, sadly, as an expert who didn't know how far away a star was, even though he'd mentioned it by name.

Drawing on my long experience of media training a number of scientists, I can tell you that they are all very keen on facts, details, accuracy and having the right answer. So, if they don't have an answer, it's not their natural instinct to reach for flannel. They live in a culture of peer review and worry a lot about what other scientists will think about what they say. This can be a big problem for many scientists in media interviews. They can find it hard to grasp that they don't have to answer media interviewers' questions exactly as they're posed.

Always be ready to build bridges

Bridging is essential if you want to maintain your authority during an interview or at a meeting. You can't be a successful spokesperson for your organisation if you don't bridge. You *must* learn to bridge easily and naturally. If you don't bridge, you'll end up stuck on the wrong side of the bridge, sinking into the mud/swamp/ deep hole/sticky stuff. If you fail to get away from talking about these hazards, at the very least you'll sound weak or defensive or it may cost you dearly and severely dent your reputation and authority.

Above my pay grade

If you're not in the C-suite and you're asked policy questions you're not comfortable answering, you can always fall back on the interview technique used by the American military when TV journalists asked them about policy decisions while they were fighting in Iraq or Afghanistan.

Interviewer: 'How long do you think you can hold out in this area?'

Military officer: 'Well, that's above my pay grade, ma'am/sir. You'll have to ask the general about that.'

The non-military version of this technique is to say something along the lines of:

'Well, I think you should ask someone on the board/more senior than me about that. That's really above my area of responsibility, so I can't comment.' Then keep going and bridge away by continuing with 'What I can tell you is that...' Of course, if you *are* in a C-suite position, you can't get away with this type of answer. You have to deal with the question in the best way you can. This should involve highly polished 'executive bridging'!

Never repeat negatives

One useful and important technique that's always worth learning is to train yourself never to repeat negatives in questions. Negative words have huge power and if you repeat them, the audience will hear them twice, so you'll have increased their power rather than diminishing it. For example, if you're asked a question like 'This is a huge problem for your company, isn't it?' you might make what seems like a normal reply, such as 'No, this isn't a huge problem'. But the problem with that reply is that the audience has now heard the negative words 'huge problem' twice and they can't stop dwelling on the negative. They may start to think 'Well, there must be a problem because they're talking about it so much'. You have to be on the alert, ready to spot negative words, and when you're asked a question with negatives in it, your reply should be a definite rebuttal, such as 'No, that's not the case...' Then make a bridge and say 'What's actually happening is...' or 'No, that's not what's happening. What we're doing is...' We repeat negatives in normal conversations in order to defeat them, so it can be hard not to do this. However, when you're a spokesperson at a meeting or you're giving a media interview, you must be aware of the power of negative words and train yourself never to repeat them. This isn't easy at first but it's well worth doing.

And finally...

The secret of success for maintaining your authority when handling difficult questions in meetings, presentations and media interviews is preparation of your messages so you always have somewhere to bridge to. This technique will help you to avoid looking rattled. People don't believe in someone who looks worried or scared. You must be able to assume a calm and confident demeanour before you start speaking and maintain this throughout your meetings and interviews. Knowing that you can make bridges will enable you to say what you want to say and look and sound confident while doing it.

Case study:
Lucy came a cropper

> One basic rule in media interviews is: don't say anything that you can't back up. Always have supporting details to hand. UK culture secretary Lucy Frazer came a cropper when she gave an interview to Sky News in January 2024 and it became clear that she couldn't provide any supporting evidence for her assertion that the BBC is biased against the government. She claimed this bias meant that the BBC risked losing the trust of its audiences and kept repeating that there was a perception among the public that the BBC

was biased. However, the interviewer, Kay Burley, repeatedly pointed out that perception is not the same as evidence. The culture secretary came across as uninformed and ineffective, which is surprising as she's a barrister by training and is used to taking on briefs and arguing her case. But she missed an opportunity to make her case against the BBC. She should have been better prepared for the obvious follow-up questions.

Chapter 7

How to handle documentary interviews

Documentaries are widespread on television channels and can cover a huge range of issues. Many are an hour long, but not all documentaries are the same. There's a wide range of different types of documentaries. Here are the main categories:

1. News and investigative – also known as current affairs.
2. Descriptive – travel, nature, historical and true crime.
3. Fly on the wall, including 'obs docs' (observational documentaries).
4. Talent led – centred around a celebrity or celebrities.
5. Reality TV – includes real people, often in competitive settings.
6. Drama documentary – a mixture of real footage and dramatised scenes.

You're more likely to be involved in numbers 1 and 3 on this list, ie current affairs documentaries and 'fly on the wall' observations of real life. An example of this is the documentary series *EasyJet: Inside the Cockpit* (2017), which followed the lives of the airline's newest pilots, plus there are many other popular series showing people at work, including police and ambulance emergency workers.

If you have expertise in travel, nature, history or crime, you might be asked to take part in category 2 as an expert, but unless you're as famous as celebrity chef Gordon Ramsay or footballer David Beckham, you're unlikely to be involved in category 4. Documentaries have become more popular with celebrities in recent years as they have come to realise the benefits of allowing cameras to follow them around and let the public into their lives 'behind the scenes'. There are numerous examples of these, from the Beckhams to Taylor Swift, whose *Taylor Swift: The Eras Tour*, released in cinemas and on Amazon Prime, has become the highest-grossing concert documentary ever made. So, it's clear why celebrities are keen on releasing documentaries about themselves. Category 5 is mostly for wannabe celebrities and there are now plenty of people who have built careers on the back of appearing in reality shows such as *The Only Way is Essex* and *Made in Chelsea*. Category 6 usually centres on historical events and uses actual footage from news reports at the time and/or actors playing people involved in specially written dramatised scenes.

TV and radio news: investigative documentary interviews

If you're interviewed for a news documentary, the important thing to remember is that you may be interviewed for a long time but that doesn't mean you'll get a lot of airtime in the broadcast. Documentary interviews are recorded and then edited – a lot. Even if you give an interview that lasts for 20 or 30 minutes, or even an hour, just one quote of less than a minute may end up in the documentary's final cut. If you're lucky, you may end up with two or three of your quotes included in the programme. I've been on both sides of the camera, making TV and radio documentary programmes and also taking part in them as an interviewee. I know what documentary producers want and how to give them quotes that I'm pretty sure they'll use. I also know why I'm taking part.

Before you take part in a documentary, you should analyse what's in it for you. What's the main message you want to get across to the public? Will it be helpful to you to give an interview to this programme? Would it be better to issue a written statement? Alternatively, will it make things look worse for you if you don't give an interview? And do you have a good story to tell that the public will sympathise with? News documentaries differ from travel, nature and historical documentaries, which usually have a presenter, experts and a voiceover. In a news documentary, your potential role is more varied. This means that, before you're interviewed for a news documentary, you need to know what your role is.

Are you a victim, an expert or a villain?

TV news documentaries investigate a topic. They provide facts and expert comment and point out problems that the reporter and producers think that we, the audience, should be concerned about. They have an agenda and set out to prove it. Those interviewed will include victims who tell us what they saw, heard and experienced, and experts who talk about their research in relevant fields. They are there to support the programme's narrative.

The third role is the villain and, clearly, unless you have an interest in representing the people or the organisation under fire, you don't want to be cast in that role. If you do have to take on the role of villain, you'll need to prepare thoroughly with carefully constructed messages that defend your position convincingly. Clearly, it's easier to be a victim or an expert. However, even in these roles, you may come under pressure to sharpen up your statements and make them more definite. You can work out before the interview how far you want to go if you're pushed. Examples of this type of programme on UK television include long-running TV documentary series such as the BBC's *Panorama*, ITV's *Tonight* and Channel 4's *Dispatches* as well as one-off programmes. In the US, *Dateline*, *Frontline* and *60 Minutes* have been broadcast for more than 40 years.

Should you issue a written statement?

It's always worth considering whether or not you should do a documentary interview. You could decide to send a short, written statement instead. The advantage of doing this is that the TV producers will probably have to use your statement in its entirety because that's all they've got from you. Also, the risks of misquoting should be zero. The disadvantages are that you may come across as avoiding the media and, if you're cast in the role of villain, this could play into the 'guilty' narrative of the documentary. The message is 'They wouldn't speak to us'. However, if you think you'll be put on the spot and can't convincingly answer tricky questions, it can be the best course of action.

Give good quotes

Remember that you're there to provide good quotes that support your role in the programme. The programme's makers are looking for interesting, clear statements that will cut through to the audience – or something vivid and colourful. They're also looking for background information from all their interviewees so that they have plenty of material to help them write the script for the programme. During your interview, the interviewer will be waiting for you to get more comfortable and then they'll try to get you to say something more interesting. However, in your terms, this could be off message. The longer the interview goes on, the more you're at risk of saying something that may be newsworthy and useful for the TV programme, but not necessarily useful for you. It's always a good idea to devote time to preparing for documentary interviews and doing practice interviews with media trainers like me, so you can ensure you're secure about what you want to say. This really pays off in terms of giving you confidence when facing a lot of questions.

Insist on a time limit

If you decide you do want to take part in a TV documentary, you should expect to prepare for a much longer interview than you'd give to a daily news programme. Documentary producers will keep on asking questions until they feel they've pushed you as far as they can in terms of giving them a good quote. So, whatever your role in a documentary, it's essential to put a time limit on your interview – and stick to it. This is harder than it sounds. If you've scheduled half an hour, the interviewer may try to keep you talking longer. One way of avoiding this is to keep your watch where you can see it so you can point out that you only have five minutes before your next meeting. However, if you ask a colleague to knock on the door or pass you a note, some producers may use this in the final cut in order to make it look as though you're not giving them enough time. Also, be careful when you sit down to start the interview or when you've finished talking. A camera may still be filming you when you think you're just chatting.

What's in your background?

It's not just what you say; it's how you look that matters in a documentary. For example, a chief executive interviewed in their boardroom with expensive-looking art on the walls behind them is going to look like a 'fat cat' and isn't going to come across as totally convincing when talking about the need to refuse pay rises, cut staff and close down factories or shops. Other background problems to watch out for are notices with distracting and negative headlines, such as 'Health and Safety', 'List of First Aid Personnel' or 'Fire Evacuation Chart'. People will be trying to read these instead of listening to what you say and your positive messages.

A documentary camera operator once told me that he felt he'd done a good job when he persuaded an executive under fire for not disposing of hazardous waste correctly to be interviewed standing outside close to waste bins. How do mistakes like this happen? It's all because the interviewee is concentrating hard on what they want to say, often in a tricky situation, so they don't notice their surroundings as much as they should. This type of mistake can be avoided if a colleague is present and they look at the setting for the interview, realise the problem and insist that the shot be altered. However always remember that if you don't like the setting for your interview you need to object before the start. Don't give the documentary makers the opportunity to say that they don't have time to reshoot your interview.

Fly on the wall documentaries

'After 20 minutes, everybody forgets about the camera.' That's what a TV documentary producer explained to me about how he got his best material. The pitch to you is that camera crews will follow you and your staff while they're working and everyone will see how you work and what wonderful work you do, and it will be great PR. My best advice is never to rush into signing up. It's a big deal and a complicated process. You have to do a lot of detailed work on what the risks and rewards are for you and your organisation. Bear in mind that everything will be recorded and then edited. You have to consider a number of important questions. How much do you trust the programme/series producers to provide a fair view of your work? Are your staff on side? You also need a good lawyer who understands the ins and outs of TV contracts. For example, will you be able to see the rushes or the rough cut? Will your comments on scripting be taken into account and will changes be made? How much control, if any, will you have over the production process?

What veto will you have on anything in the final version? What fees/repeat fees will you get?

The very first fly on the wall documentary on British TV dates back to the 1970s. In April 1974, the BBC began broadcasting a series of programmes called *The Family*. It showed the life of the Wilkins, an ordinary working-class family from Reading. The BBC website now describes this series as 'raising controversial issues about class, race and manners in 1970s England', and it was 'the first time that cameras had simply filmed daily life without direct interviews'. Since then, this genre of broadcasting has grown steadily. TV schedules around the world have included numerous examples of fly on the wall TV programmes. They're now also known as 'obs docs' – short for observational documentaries. In their purest form, they don't have voiceover narration, but many series nowadays will use the voice of a narrator to keep the audience interested. Here are some examples you may have watched: *Traffic Cops*, *Police 24/7*, *Inside the Ambulance*, *UK Border Force* (also USA and Australia), *EasyJet: Inside the Cockpit* and *Inside the Tower of London*, among many others. It's important to note that these programmes can now have long lives. They may be repeated on the huge variety of TV channels that are now available as well as on streaming services. This means that, if you do decide to take part in this type of programme, you should think carefully about what sort of content you're happy to see on air – for years to come.

Case study:
Inside the Tower of London

The British TV broadcaster Channel 5 has had a hit with its series of documentaries called *Inside the Tower of London*. It provides fascinating access to the day-to-day lives and challenges of the people who live and work at the historic landmark. Built in the 1070s by William I, the Tower of London is a world-famous tourist attraction. It has its ravens and Beefeaters, more properly known as Yeomen Warders, as well as a long history of royal apartments, the Crown Jewels, executions, imprisonments and torture. Laura Hutchinson, head of media and PR for Historic Royal Palaces, which manages the Tower of London, told me the documentary series has definitely had an impact on visitor numbers. 'In the summer of 2023, 18 per cent of visitors said they were prompted to visit the Tower by seeing the TV series,' she said. 'So, it outperformed our marketing campaign. When we've been filming, visitors have come up to the Yeomen Warders and told them they love the series and that's why they've come to the Tower. Historic Royal Palaces lost a lot of money during the lockdowns, but we kept on filming when we could. We did the first two series before the first lockdown, Series 3 in lockdown, Series 4 while we were getting back to normal and Series 5 and 6 after lockdown. My advice to anyone looking into whether or not to go ahead with a documentary series about their organisation is first to take great care in selecting the production company. Don't be seduced by the glamour of the producers promising you the world by being on TV. Don't go for the first one that approaches you. We looked at a number of companies and got them to make taster tapes so we could see what sort of tone they were taking. We also looked at their output online.

'We deal with production companies all the time because we're often used as a filming location, so we had lots of previous experience, including dealing with health and safety – and we have a full-time filming officer. Filming *Inside the Tower of London* takes up a lot of staff time. It takes about 50 hours of filming for each one-hour episode. You can't direct the production but you can influence it by allocating a member of staff to aid and observe all filming. You've also got to brief staff members and make sure all your spokespeople are familiar with what's happening in terms of filming.

'I've learned a lot since we started and the contract has evolved. We do a two-week pre-planning phase, which is built into the contract. Also, I ask for episode summaries with storylines. The tension is that you want to control everything the film crew do, but this would make it too PR and bland. We don't know everything they are going to say in the programmes, but we know what they want. We do get to see the cut before the final cut. It's in the contract that we can check for factual accuracy and security factors. It's a respectful relationship on both sides.'

When I asked Laura if she had any regrets, she

said that on just one occasion someone at the Tower had 'gone off piste' – but it didn't make it into the programme, so it all worked out well. 'It's a really big, engaged audience and for us it's been a massive benefit. The only downside is the amount of work you have to put into it.'

Reality TV programmes

Fly on the wall documentaries are not to be confused with reality TV shows that use a documentary format with voiceover. In reality TV, ordinary people are selected because they can be cast in different roles by the programme's producers and events are staged or competitions imposed to create entertainment. The term 'docusoap' has been used for many documentary-style reality television shows. Examples include *Big Brother*, *Love Island*, *The Apprentice* and the *Real Housewives* franchise, and, of course, the huge worldwide success that is *Keeping Up with the Kardashians*. If you take part in this type of show, either as a 'contestant', as a supplier of goods or providing a venue that the 'stars' visit, you'll be well advised to have an agent representing you, or to acquire one before you sign up to take part.

You'll need to work out why you want to take part and remember that this type of show can generate huge publicity but this can be negative as well as positive. Some reality TV stars people have built businesses and careers as minor celebrities having first come to public attention in reality TV programmes. While they're in a show, they can build huge followings on social media and become influencers doing paid posts, promotions and collaborations with brands. They can go on to write books and appear on other reality shows.

Case studies: Reality TV success stories

Georgia Toffalo has a degree in politics and started her TV career by appearing in *Made in Chelsea* in 2014 while working as head of events for a think tank called Parliament Street. She went on to win the UK version of *I'm a Celebrity... Get Me Out of Here!* in 2017. She has also appeared on various other TV shows including *Celebrity Hunted* and *This Morning*. She has had best-selling romantic novels published by Mills and Boon and an autobiography. She has 1.8 million followers on Instagram, where she promotes Wildpack, her business selling raw food for dogs. She's reported to have a net worth of £5 million and promotes herself as leading a millionaire lifestyle. She was the face of fashion brand Shein, and had three collections with the company before cutting ties after a Channel 4 documentary found some workers were only being paid 3p per clothing item produced.

Gemma Collins began appearing in *The Only Way is Essex* in 2011, as a car salesperson. She now has more than two million followers on Instagram and styles herself as 'Gemma Clair Collins – I don't need an introduction'. She too has published books, including an autobiography, and calls herself 'The GC'. She has campaigned against animal testing and took part in *Celebrity Big Brother* and other TV shows. She also fronted her own reality show called *Diva Forever*, which followed her everyday life. She appears in the media telling her fans about her love life with her different fiancés, her weight loss and her expensive holidays abroad. She's well known for being calamity prone, most famously when she fell over when appearing in Celebrity Dancing on Ice. Despite this dizzy image she's reported to have made more than £7 million from her reality show career.

Reality TV show positives

As these two case studies and those of many other reality TV stars illustrate, it is possible to make real money by using reality TV show appearances to become famous and build your business or businesses. Providing you're prepared to go all in, in terms of what you're prepared to do on TV and then also keeping your lifestyle under the spotlight online, you can become wealthy. But you have to give a lot to get a lot.

Reality TV show negatives

Not everyone can live with the pressures of instant fame, as the suicides of three *Love Island* contestants and one of the programme's former presenters, Caroline Flack, have sadly shown (Belcher 2021). ITV subsequently increased the mental health support for contestants on the show. A quick glance at the internet will throw up numerous articles listing complaints from reality TV show participants, some of whom say they had to have treatment for depression after their appearances on shows that promised them fame and fortune (Saner 2019). The stark reality is that both social and traditional media thrive on comments about people who appear on reality TV programmes, leading to huge numbers of negative as well as positive personal comments, so you need to be sure you're the right person to appear on this type of programme before you enter the selection process. It's also advisable to look online and find an agent who can steer your career and protect you from the huge and very real challenges that reality TV inevitably brings.

Chapter 8

The power of podcasting

Podcasts are the perfect example of the fact that we're all broadcasters now. Their appeal lies not just in the huge choice of content, which can be listened to – and increasingly watched – anytime, anywhere, but also in the fact that anyone can set up a podcast with basic equipment. This is in stark contrast to broadcasting, where the broadcasters are the gatekeepers who control output. The number of podcasts has been rising steadily ever since the first episodes emerged in the early 2000s. They are now big business, generating advertising revenue of more than $1 billion a year.

The word podcast comes from a combination of iPod and broadcast. Podcasts started to appear in 2003 on audio only and were a form of online radio that could be played on the iPod mp3 player. In 2005, podcast was made word of the year by the *New Oxford American Dictionary* and in the same year, George W Bush became the first president to deliver a weekly address in podcast form. Podcasts moved on to iTunes and YouTube and video podcasts have become increasingly popular, with YouTube the top source for finding podcasts. If you're taking part in a podcast, you need to treat it as part of the visual economy and make sure your appearance is appropriately professional. See my advice in Chapter 4.

According to Podcast Index, in 2024 there were an estimated 4.1 million active podcasts. Spotify and Apple Podcasts are the biggest players; Spotify claims to have 4.7 million podcasts on its platform while Apple has 2.5 million (data from 2023). Some podcasts appear on both platforms. Podcasts are available in more than 100 different languages although more than 60 per cent are in English.

In recent data shared by Exploding Topics (Howarth 2024), almost two thirds of Americans over the age of 12 have listened to a podcast, with young people listening twice as much as the over-55s. More than 100 million people in the US alone listen to a podcast every month and just under 80 million watched podcasts on video. Countries in which podcasting is growing fast include Chile, Argentina, Peru, Mexico and China. Research by RAJAR, the official body for measuring radio audiences in the UK, shows that a third of UK adults are listening to podcasts every month and the figures are rising.

Advertisers don't waste their money on media platforms that bring them no financial returns, so podcasts are becoming increasingly influential in the media landscape. According to podcast research company Edison Media Research, the average podcast listener is young, wealthy, educated, employed full time, uses social media and follows brands on it, subscribes to on-demand video services and nearly always listens to whole episodes, creating an intimate bond between host and listener.

Joe Rogan is the richest and most listened-to podcaster in the world, with 200 million listeners (Wilson

2024). As the BBC website reported in 2022, Spotify is thought to have paid more than $100m (£74 million) for exclusive rights to the *The Joe Rogan Experience* podcast in 2020. It's now the top podcast on Spotify and is reportedly downloaded almost 200 million times a month.

How to become a podcast guest

Not everyone wants to be or can be a guest on Joe Rogan's podcast but there are millions of other podcasts to choose from, covering a huge variety of topics. To find out which of these will be good for you and your area of expertise, you need to do some research.

There are various ways to become a podcast guest:

- ✦ contact podcast hosts directly
- ✦ use a guest placement service
- ✦ promote yourself as available for podcast interviews on LinkedIn and on your website and wait for creators to reach out
- ✦ follow a combination of all these strategies.

It can take a while to get traction, but once you've started appearing on a few podcasts, more opportunities are likely to come up. Note that podcast guests aren't usually paid – the benefit comes through exposure. And appearances of this kind act as powerful social proof of your expertise and thought leadership. Likewise, podcast appearances can be great marketing for brands seeking an engaged and targeted audience.

Guidance for giving successful podcast interviews

Podcast interviews are usually less confrontational than news interviews – and they're often long and conversational. But don't let this fool you into thinking this means they're easy to do well. You need to take these interviews seriously and prepare thoroughly. Many a news story has come out of a chatty podcast interview where the interviewee relaxed and gave too much away or said something embarrassing about their personal life that they later regretted. Podcast comments can lead to social media comments and, if you slip up, you may go viral and be picked up by the tabloid media, which now relies on a steady diet of stories about 'podcast slip-ups', 'Twitter spats' or 'Instagram shame'.

Even in a lengthy podcast interview, it's a good idea to make headline statements that will stick in people's minds. You'll have much longer to talk about why you've made these statements and what justifies them, but this doesn't mean you should be woolly or fuzzy about your agenda-setting statements. The best podcasts are full of stories with headlines that audiences remember. Listen and learn and think about how you can select and tell anecdotes that will bring your messages to life and be memorable for the right reasons.

Take time to prepare

As with all other types of media interviews, preparation is the key to success. Always prepare a lot of material for a long interview and check yourself before telling any unprepared jokes or funny stories. If you say something like 'Well, I've never told anyone this before, but...', your audience perks up, some people will post about it and journalists may pick it up. If you do want to say something you've never said before, make sure it reflects well on you and your organisation and is something you'd be happy to see in print, on TV or on social media. Whether you're giving a long interview or a short one, the same advice applies as I've given in Chapter 6 about making the most of your media interviews. Make sure you set aside a minimum of an hour to prepare so you can be clear about what you want to discuss. Bridging is important here, as the range of questions can be very wide indeed.

Where can you do a podcast interview?

There are a variety of settings for podcast interviews. These are:

- in a radio studio, where you meet the interviewer in person
- in a podcast studio, where you meet the interviewer in person
- in your office or at home, where you meet the interviewer in person
- online via your computer, phone or tablet.

Questions to ask before your podcast interview:

- How and where do they want you to do the interview?
- Is it live or pre-recorded?
- Will it be videoed?
- Do they want you to wear headphones or not?
- What time do they want to talk to you?

- ✦ How long should you allow for the podcast interview?
- ✦ Will there be a pre-meeting either on the phone or online to discuss the questions?
- ✦ Have you listened to this podcast?
- ✦ Do you know the sort of approach/tone they take?
- ✦ Have they sent you a description of what they do and why?
- ✦ Do they have a 'funny' question they always ask at the end of the interview in order to leave the audience on a light note?

Case study: The podcast producer

Here's an edited email from a podcast producer, which illustrates the fact that you need to devote time to preparing both yourself and your equipment for your podcast interviews. It's not the same as doing a phone interview.

Dear *Name*

We are so excited to have you on podcast this week – *date and time*.

Link: Here is your link to join the Zoom meeting.

The first 15 minutes is to walk you through the recording. Then the host will read out the introduction and start interviewing someone else on the same topic. At this point, you will be muted but you can listen in. After that interview, you will be interviewed.

I will go through a short checklist before the recording to make sure everything is set up

correctly, but please note the list below to ensure good audio quality:
- If possible, use an ethernet cable to connect to the internet.
- ALWAYS wear headphones.
- Make sure all notifications are turned off on your computer.
- Make sure your phone is on airplane mode.
- Have your laptop/computer connected to its charger.
- Please set up in a room without echoing or other background noise (small room, ideally).

Please note you'll be able to see your host on the video screen while we are recording. We will not be using the video. Finally, please sign and return the attached release form.

Please send a headshot we can use online.

Do contact me with any questions you might have.

Will your podcast be on video as well as audio?

The podcast in the case study above won't be on video, but you should never assume this to be the case. Always check whether you'll be on video or not. Even if a video won't be recorded, the podcaster may wish to use a screenshot of you for their publicity so you should always look neat and tidy. Unless you're promoting sleepwear or leisurewear or you're an influencer promoting your home life as part of your image, don't wear pyjamas! (Refer to Chapter 4's advice on appearance.)

Setting up your own podcast

Setting up and running your own podcast takes work but it can be valuable in terms of establishing your brand and building your business.

Your podcast checklist:

Step 1 – Define your concept and your target audience

- Who do you want to appeal to?
- What are your areas of expertise?
- What topics do you want to talk about?

Step 2 – Content forward planning

- Be organised. Plan each episode. Create a content calendar for the next year. If you want to have interviewees once a month, make a list of the people you want to talk to and when. Have your content worked out for the first three months minimum and add significant topics or events with fixed dates such as major trade shows and conferences. Draw up your release schedule and stick to it. To build up and retain your audience, you should be consistent in how and when you release your podcasts and trail them.

Step 3 – Recording equipment

- It's essential to have good quality audio for your podcast. Invest in a good microphone, headphones and audio recording and editing software. As discussed above, many podcasts are on video as well as audio. Will you be filming your podcast? If the answer is yes, you need to consider investing in a broadcast-quality video camera.

Step 4 – Select your podcast hosting platform

- You can launch your podcast for free on RSS.com.
- An RSS feed is a unique URL that allows podcast directories such as Apple and Spotify to access and display your episodes. You can also use YouTube or Vimeo to release your video podcasts.
- According to Wix (Sernoff 2023), the best hosting sites are: Wix Podcast Player, Podbean, Buzzsprout, Libsyn, Spreaker, Simplecast, Transistor, Blubrry, Captivate, Castos, Audioboom, SoundCloud, Anchor, Megaphone and Podcast Websites. Meanwhile Acast describes itself as 'the home of podcasting' with 100,000 podcasts listened more than 430 million times every month in total.

Step 5 – Recording and editing

- You must have a quiet place in which to record your podcasts. You can set this up yourself at your office or home, or book time in a professional recording studio. Many studios offer discounted rates for podcast recordings, especially in the evening.
- There are several free editing software options for beginners, which enable you to edit out background noise and ensure consistent volume levels throughout your recording. You can also add music or sound effects if you want to. The best known are Audacity and GarageBand, which is available free if you have an Apple device. Both have free advice online on how to use them.

Step 6 – Cover art

- Take the time to design visually appealing podcast cover art that reflects your podcast theme. This will be the first thing your listeners and potential listeners see, so it needs to align with your brand.

Step 7 – Setting up on your hosting platform

- Your hosting platform will give you instructions on how to upload your episodes. You will also be required to write descriptions of your episodes and set your release schedules. Always double check to make sure that your details are accurate and your cover art is attractive. This includes double checking your title and descriptions.

Step 8 – Podcast directories

- Submit your podcast to major directories such as Apple, Spotify and Google. Each has its own guidelines that need to be followed. Putting your podcast on the directories will help you build up your audience.

Step 9 – Promoting your podcast

- You can use social media and your website to promote your podcast. Always ask for feedback, engage with your audience and encourage your listeners to share your episodes. If you want to build up a base of dedicated listeners and viewers, you need to publish and promote your episodes consistently.

Step 10 – Analyse

- Review the analytics provided by your hosting platform and podcast directories. You can find out who your audience are, what topics they like the most and tailor your content to your audience's preferences.

Finally – always be consistent. Working hard on your podcast can pay dividends in terms of boosting your business.

How to make money from your podcast

According to Statista.com, the podcast advertising market worldwide is anticipated to witness significant growth, with projected revenue reaching $4.02 billion in 2024. By 2027, the market is expected to exhibit a steady annual growth rate of 7.76 per cent, resulting in a projected market volume of $5.03 billion. Joe Rogan is reported to make $800,000 per episode, but of course not all podcasters achieve that level of turnover. You can, however, build up your podcast business by using a number of the most popular revenue streams. According to podcast creators Descript (Romanoff 2023), the main effective ways to make money podcasting are:

- ✦ using podcast advertising networks
- ✦ brand sponsorships
- ✦ affiliate marketing
- ✦ merchandise sales
- ✦ listener donations and crowdfunding
- ✦ premium content
- ✦ live shows and events
- ✦ email lists
- ✦ syndicating your podcast
- ✦ book sales

- offering consulting and coaching services
- paid podcast subscriptions.

In other words, you need to do some research and business planning and work out the best ways for you to make money from your podcast and incorporate it into your marketing.

How do I get my first guest on my podcast?

To attract your first podcast guest, you could:

- use your own contacts and book an expert you already know or know of
- pay a monthly fee to register on podcast guest placement services such as PodMatch
- look on LinkedIn for experts in your podcast field and send them invites
- search podcast directories such as Apple Podcasts then contact suitable guests directly.

Case study: Style Stories

> Lisa Gillbe is a style consultant and personal shopper who presents her own podcast called Style Stories, aimed at women over 40. She has 1,000–2,000 listeners per episode with an audience in the UK, Australia, New Zealand and the US. She describes her podcast like this:
>
> 'The Style Stories podcast is here to solve all your style and wardrobe dilemmas. Highly experienced London-based personal stylist Lisa Gillbe brings wardrobe tips and tricks that make sure you get a

capsule wardrobe that really works for you. This advice will get you thinking differently about your style and image so you can feel inspired, confident and excited about your wardrobe.'

Lisa started podcasting in 2018 and, as an example of how you can be interviewed anywhere for a podcast, she interviewed me for her first podcast series in a café at the Institute of Directors in central London, using her smartphone. She says it all started when a friend told her that, as she was always talking about fashion and style, she should do a podcast. 'I said oh no, I don't think I can do that, but she got her phone out, downloaded an app and we started talking. To start with it was just me and some friends chatting without much structure and it was all a bit ramshackle. However, I soon realised I needed to do more planning and include some interviews with experts, not just chats. I changed the title to Style Stories and I aim to do two or three podcasts per month. Each podcast takes at least a day and a half in total time spent. That includes preparation of the topic and, if there's an interviewee, sending them the plan for the content. The style is conversational and relaxed, and it does evolve while recording, but you need structure in order to get the most out of the topic. Then it takes one hour for the recording, two hours for the editing and more time for writing and sending the mailing and the show notes.

'I use a Blue Snowball microphone and record on Riverside FM, the online podcast recording service. I then edit it in Podcastle, using the free editing service, and broadcast it using Podbean, which automatically shares it on all major podcast platforms, such as Apple and Spotify. All this costs less than

£30 a month, as I use the free services as much as possible.

You can pay more and use AI to write your show notes, which saves time. My podcasts are a mixture of audio and visual and I share the videos on YouTube.'

Here's Lisa's advice to new podcasters:

- Prepare a list of topics and record a few episodes before you launch so you can release them in one go. This means that people can binge-listen right from the start and it helps get you up the charts.
- Listen to your audience. Ask them what content they want to hear and create episodes around that. I have a Facebook group and I ask them what topics they want me to talk about. For example, I ask them, 'What are your wardrobe woes?' Asking the audience is so useful because it gives me lots of material that I know people are keen to hear about.
- Give shout-outs to people who take the time to leave reviews. Always ask for reviews and for people to subscribe to your podcast.
- Use the podcast to grow your email list. The podcast helps me to have something valuable to share across social media, and when people join my Facebook group they have to sign up with their email. I get clients from my podcast because it raises my profile. Podcasting positions you as an authority in your field and gives you a platform to share your expertise. It's a great way for people to get to know you and feel confident about booking your services. I get contacts from across the world.

Chapter 9

Building your profile online using free or inexpensive media

Working from home has resulted in a huge growth in remote meetings and interviews, whether media or job interviews. It has also created huge opportunities for looking like an amateur on TV or on video. Why? Because whether you're talking from your home or your office, when you use your computer, tablet or smartphone, you're the producer and the director. When you go to a TV studio to give an interview, highly trained people are there to make sure the picture, the lighting and the sound are all professionally delivered. You only have to worry about your content, your performance and your appearance.

However, when you're talking from your home or an office, it's much more challenging than going to a studio where professional technicians will sort out your lighting and framing. In fact, it's an entirely different situation. Why? Because you are in charge of your image and all the technical stuff. There are no experts to help you. So, as well as delivering your interview content with authority, making sure your appearance is smart and conquering your nerves, you have to ensure that you look good on-screen. This means following my advice in Chapter 3 on assessing and adjusting your framing, background, lighting and sound, as well as checking your appearance and avoiding interruptions from children, pets and colleagues.

The exponential growth of social media in the 21st century means that there have never been more opportunities for you to build your reputation without spending a fortune. You can create free or inexpensive social media profiles on LinkedIn, Instagram, X (formerly Twitter), TikTok, Snapchat and Facebook as well as others. The visual economy dominates on all these platforms. Market research consistently shows that using videos and static images in your posts will generate more impact, with more impressions, likes and comments. According to LinkedIn, posts that feature videos and static images get higher responses than posts using text alone.

You have the tools in your smartphone to create your own images and videos – but you need to plan to take advantage of this technology. You also need to behave like a broadcaster. You have to think of good stories and headline discussion points that you can post about and, when you attend a business event, you need to report on your own life with pictures and videos. Social media really does mean that we are all broadcasters now and that involves taking the time to take pictures and selfies and get someone else to take pictures of you with important people. Then you need to write something about it! This doesn't happen by magic; it takes work to do it well.

How to build a personal brand on social media

It's the big question for many people: how do I raise my profile online? And then there are other questions, such as: how do I come across as an expert and not as a show-off? What sort of things can I comment on? How can I use thought leadership to build my credibility? What are the best ways to build my personal brand to help my career? You may not realise it, but even if you think you don't, you already have a personal brand. People who do business with you already have an opinion about you. When you work on building your personal brand, your main aims will be to make yourself memorable for the right reasons and to stand out from the crowd of people in your field as someone who's knowledgeable, trustworthy and a person people would like to work with.

As personal branding expert Jennifer Holloway puts it in her bestselling book *Personal Branding for Brits* (2013), 'hiding your light under a bushel is no longer the canniest thing to do: people who want to move their career to the next stage; people who realise they can't do their job until they've got buy-in from their team; people who understand their personal brand is their company brand; people who are leaders of tomorrow establishing their credentials today – whatever reason you have for wanting to work on your personal brand, they're all underpinned by one primary rule: people buy people.' Her message is that if you don't build a personal brand, you'll be left behind.

You can't separate the personal from the professional

The most important piece of advice to take on board when using social media is always to be careful and thoughtful about what you post. It's essential to understand that everything matters and can live online forever. In practice, this means that it's not advisable to have a contrast between your personal social media and your business postings. Remember that the media pack are always looking for stories and they find a lot of them on social media. Some people have come unstuck in the media when they've posted personal views that don't align with their work posts and the views and policies of their organisations. This doesn't mean you can't, for example, have a personal Facebook account – but don't open it up to everyone and always think about the price you might pay if you post photos of yourself after a few drinks, sticking out your tongue or in other undignified poses.

Remember that even if an account is private, people can repost or share what you put in a private group. Nothing that appears online is totally private and secure. This advice also applies to WhatsApp. You may be posting to a select group of your friends, family or work colleagues, but never forget that although your group is encrypted, what you put on WhatsApp can be reposted elsewhere to a wider audience. TikTok stories may disappear after 24 hours but, in that time, they can be downloaded and shared.

Experts on using LinkedIn for business, and there are many of them, usually advise that it's better to post on your personal page to establish your personal brand. This doesn't mean personal as in your personal life. This means your personal professional brand, which means your personal

LinkedIn page is a business page. This is the practice I've followed for several years and I now have more than 3,000 followers. I post a mixture of my own blogs (at least once a month) with advice about handling the media and the visual economy issues highlighted in this book, as well as sharing relevant news stories about communications and media interviews, both positive and negative. I also post about media training issues, media interviews that I do myself and business events I attend with pictures of myself and others. Some of these posts are also posted on my company page, TV News London, as well as Instagram, Facebook Business and X (formerly Twitter). I have more followers than the company page and that's how it should be when you're building and maintaining your personal brand. A company page will tend to be more formal and less interesting than a personal one. It's so easy to be overlooked in today's fast-moving business world and regular posting on LinkedIn ensures that people won't forget you. This isn't just marketing. I look at this as a form of online networking and always post videos or static images, which can receive anything between 500 and 3,000 views. Interestingly, the most views I've ever had for a LinkedIn post was more than 25,000 for a post with pictures about the first newsreader in New Zealand with a Māori tattoo on her face, reading the main nightly news. This turned out to be of interest across the world!

Beware social media posts that incur penalties

As long ago as 2014, the BBC website carried an article reporting that one in ten job seekers between the ages of 16 and 34 had been rejected for a job because of something they'd posted online. Careers advisors routinely advise students to clean up their social media when they start applying for jobs. Recruiters check up on job applicants by looking at their social media accounts and if they find images or text that they consider inappropriate, such as someone's views on religion and politics, criticisms of their current boss or ex-partners, insults and feuds with ex-friends, bad behaviour or slacking off at work, lots of swearing, nudity or pictures of drunken parties, it can cost them a job offer or an actual job. Over-posting can also raise red flags as it can make you appear more committed to your social media profile than your career. You're not a celebrity – you don't need to post every day.

Checklist for building your personal brand

- ✦ Who are your target audience?
- ✦ What do they want to know?
- ✦ You have to give to get – what advice can you give to establish yourself as an expert?
- ✦ Make a list of topics you want to write blogs about that will give value and establish you as a thought leader in your field.
- ✦ Look out for articles and other posts on these topics to repost or write about.
- ✦ Post about your webinars and other events and offers.
- ✦ List the business events you're going to attend and then post about them.
- ✦ Decide how much personal information, if any, you want to share.
- ✦ Check LinkedIn every day so you can keep up with comments on your posts.

- Always drive people to your company website and make sure you improve your SEO (search engine optimisation) with keywords and phrases that your audience will search for.
- Keep up with the latest developments on your social media platforms. There's plenty of free advice to help you make sure you're not missing out on new opportunities.
- As part of your strategy for building your personal brand, make your own videos and read the advice on this in the next chapter.
- To further establish yourself as an expert, consider writing a book. You can then produce a lot of visual material for your website and social media posts with pictures of you and your book. You could also use it as a resource for webinars or to gain speaking engagements, either online or in person.

How not to do it on social media

In 2016, Angela Gibbins was the head of global estates at the British Council, which promotes British culture in more than 200 countries and is a public body sponsored by the British government. She was dismissed from her job in August that year after comments she made on Facebook appeared in *The Sun*. It all started with a photo of the then three-year-old Prince George, posted by the band Dub Pistols on their Facebook page, with an extremely insulting caption. Underneath the image and the caption, Ms Gibbins commented: 'White privilege. That cheeky grin is the (already locked-in) innate knowledge that he is royal, rich, advantaged and will never know *any* difficulty or hardships in life. Let's find photos of 3yo Syrian refugee children and see if they look alike, eh?' Ms Gibbins believed her comments were only visible to her Facebook friends but they were passed on to *The Sun* newspaper and prompted extensive criticism of the charity and calls for her to leave. An internal investigation found that Ms Gibbins had unwittingly breached the British Council's code of conduct and brought it into disrepute. She contested her dismissal and took the Council to an employment tribunal on the grounds of wrongful dismissal and discrimination against her republican beliefs. The tribunal rejected her claims and said she had been fired because there had been 'gross misconduct' in posting the comments and she had 'associated herself with a distasteful and personal attack on a small child'.

In 2009, the 'lying down game', also known as 'planking', swept across the world. It involved people lying flat, face down on their stomachs in public places including roads and pavements, luggage racks, supermarket checkout conveyor belts and many other unlikely spots. Seven doctors and nurses on a night shift at the A&E department at Swindon's Great Western Hospital in Wiltshire joined in and posted pictures of each other lying face down on resuscitation trolleys, on ward floors and on the Wiltshire air ambulance helipad. Hospital bosses were not impressed. They asked Facebook to remove the posts and suspended seven medics on full pay pending disciplinary hearings for unprofessional conduct.

In 2008, Virgin Atlantic sacked 13 staff after they made critical comments on Facebook, including claims that there were cockroaches on some of its planes and some of the fleet's engines were poor quality and dangerous. They also criticised passengers. Virgin Atlantic said in a statement that the staff had broken their contracts by bringing the company into disrepute and that other avenues were available to them for airing grievances. 'There is a time and a place for Facebook. But there is no justification for it to be used as a sounding board for staff of any company to criticise the very passengers who ultimately pay their salaries.'

It's worth pointing out that I found all these negative examples and others online, some with names and details that are still haunting the people who made these career damaging mistakes.

Creating useful social media content

This takes planning and constant vigilance. It's important to regard all your social media as part of your personal brand, so you need to keep it professional. This doesn't mean you can't have any fun with your friends and colleagues but always remember that nothing online is ever completely and safely private. Keep in mind the examples of bad judgement above and always think twice before you post anything. Never post when you're angry or after consuming alcohol. These are good policies and should mean you avoid posting something that damages your reputation, could get you fired or offends your clients. Asking a colleague to check your content before posting on your business accounts is also good practice.

Whether you're in a large or a small team, it's vital to understand the type of content you're looking for and the tone you want to take. You need to be clear and consistent in what you and your team are posting. You should always aim for content that demonstrates your professionalism and knowledge of your field. You want people to know, trust and respect you and ultimately want to do business with you or recommend you to someone else. Useful content includes:

- blogs on business and professional issues by you or your colleagues
- reports by your organisation
- media releases by your organisation
- media articles in your field you can link to and comment on
- events you attend, such as conferences, trade shows, exhibitions, networking meetings, prize-givings, formal dinners and lunches
- posting, reposting or commenting on relevant content by other professionals
- posting or reposting wise sayings that appeal to your audience
- asking questions and starting a debate about a business issue
- asking questions for input about a topic you want to blog about.

Don't be tempted to spend all your time talking about yourself. While it's important and useful to build your personal brand and make yourself more interesting to your audience, social media experts advise that your ratio for business postings should be 3:1 for original content. This means that for every post about yourself, you should create three posts that may include you but are about someone or something relevant to your audience and your field of expertise.

Case study: Lynne Parker

Funny Women, which launched in 2003 to promote the careers of female comedians in the UK, now gets more than 2,000 applications for the annual Funny Women Awards. This contrasts with 2003, when they had only 70 entrants for one award. Founder Lynne Parker says: 'Great social media content takes time and effort to produce and I'm guilty of letting updates slip down the priority list. However, perfection isn't necessary and it's good to shape your output around news, opinions and external events as well as your own activities. I trained as a journalist quite a few years ago now, before the advent of social media, when the world was a very different place. Content was printed and all articles or features were looked over by editors before publication. Now that we can publish anything ourselves, my advice would be to get somebody else to look over your content before you unleash it on the world, especially if it's important for your business or personal profile.'

Decide which social media platforms work for you

You don't have to post on every platform. For business posts, many people use LinkedIn, Facebook Business, X and Instagram. You can post text, static images and video on all these platforms and collect followers who will look out for your posts. If you're selling physical products, Pinterest, Snapchat and TikTok are more useful. To succeed on TikTok you can start by making videos aimed at a young audience, usually lasting a minute or less, and you can graduate to longer videos to create a community of devoted followers. You can find advice in the next chapter about how to make videos using your phone.

Keep your social media profiles up to date

LinkedIn is the most important social media platform for many businesses but, despite this, there are some people who don't have a picture of themselves on their profile. If you want people to engage with you, include a recent photo of yourself. You also need to put some images in the banner behind your photo. Leaving it plain and pale grey makes it seem as if you don't really care. Keep all your social media information up to date and post regularly to maintain your profile on all the platforms you're using.

Write your own statement and include keywords for your field of expertise. People want to know who you are, what you do and why. You want to stand out as above average. Always make sure the pictures on your social media home pages are the same simple headshot. Avoid using a mid-shot (taken from a middle distance) or a wide shot or, even worse, wearing party or beach clothes, posing in a bar or on holiday. Unprofessional photos also include those that are blurry, have bad lighting or include other people. And yes, I've seen examples of all these mistakes. Remember that many people will look you up on their phones, and if they can't see a clear headshot, they may not want to engage with you. Many people follow a policy of not connecting with anyone who doesn't have a picture on their profile, so making sure your photo looks professional is vitally important.

LinkedIn is routinely used by both recruiters and jobseekers, so if you don't look well presented and you're not using up to date information, you may lose out on being hired or on hiring the best people for your organisation. Journalists also look to LinkedIn and other social media for information about people they're interviewing. Start off by posting at least once a week. If you suddenly don't post for a few weeks, people may unfollow you. If, for example, the message 'Jane hasn't posted recently' pops up on LinkedIn, you'll look the opposite of dynamic.

Making connections

If someone contacts you out of the blue on LinkedIn, you have to decide whether or not to connect with them. If you've met them, they're colleagues in the same organisation or you have a lot of connections in common, you'll probably decide to connect. If you don't know them, you can check whether they have any of the same connections and make a decision on that basis. Try to spot people who are only going to contact you with sales pitches. Do you want to completely avoid them, or do you think they're worth networking with as potential clients?

To help you grow your network, LinkedIn has a 'People you may know' feature, which suggests suitable connections based on interests, workplaces or other experiences you have in common, as well as contacts imported from your address books. You need to decide on an individual basis which of these contacts could be useful to you.

Once you've made a new connection, you can decide to send a message thanking them for connecting. You can tell them what you do and suggest how you could be useful to them and invite them to an event or to meet you in person or online. Your aim is to build connections with your audience and create relationships with long-term loyalty. By sharing content that invites your audience into your working life, sharing some personal interests and responding to comments and messages, you can build a community around your brand and create a bond that goes beyond just a transactional relationship. LinkedIn provides a lot of useful advice about how to get started and it's a good idea to take advantage of this. You can also pay to use LinkedIn Premium or Sales Navigator for more access to potential marketing targets.

If you mention another person or company on social media, remember to look up their account and tag it. Tagging a brand or a person can be the first step in building a new relationship and it will greatly increase your chances of a repost and greater reach to a wider audience.

Building your community

Quantity or quality? Who are your target audience? Will you be better off with 100 followers, 1,000 or 10,000? You have to work this out in terms of your own marketing strategy. You also need to decide which social media platforms you want to focus on. Choose the platform that's going to be the best choice for you by looking at other people's posts. You don't need to be on every social media platform but it all helps to keep up your SEO on Google. It's important to help people find you online. If you're not coming up on the first or second pages of a Google search, you're not doing well. Only an investigative journalist or a competitor is going to plough through more pages to find you and neither of them is interested in paying you! You can get advice on SEO from Google.

Responding to comments on social media

Posting is a two-way street. Don't let people feel you aren't listening to them when they've taken the time to comment on your posts – but be careful not to argue. 'Agree to disagree' is the wisest approach. On X, you may receive more negative comments than on other platforms, depending on who you follow. It's often the best course of action to ignore provocative comments. The delete button is your friend – you can block or report hate speech or irrelevant spam. You may also decide that X is not appropriate for your organisation.

Emojis and abbreviations have rapidly developed into separate languages. Many have meanings known only to young people and, unless you know them well, you can come unstuck in emails and other messages. If you do use them in business communications, you really do need to know what they mean.

When he was the UK's prime minister, David Cameron was embarrassed when he was reported to have used the acronym 'LOL' on his messages to friends, thinking it meant 'lots of love' when it actually means 'laugh out loud'. *The Guardian* newspaper (O'Carroll 2012) reported that a member of the House of Lords revealed that DC, as he was known, had sent him a message of condolence after his father died and ended the message with LOL. The lesson is never assume you know what abbreviations or acronyms mean. Also, be aware of context. Abbreviations can be useful and efficient in informal email writing and messages but even widely used abbreviations are not appropriate for business-related social media posts. Not everyone will know what they mean and they can detract from your expert image. Use sentences and phrases in your posts rather than abbreviations.

Conversational language is acceptable but don't be too casual. Acronyms and technical terms need to be spelled out because otherwise many in your audience will feel baffled and excluded. And many more of them will be baffled by emojis. Emojis can be a minefield all of their own and new ones are being introduced all the time. Even positive emojis such as smiley faces can appear inappropriate and there are lots of different smiley emojis, all with different meanings. Keeping up with the meanings of emojis isn't something that most of us can spare the time to do. Finally, of course, always avoid using any emojis that are too casual or childish for a work setting, such as those featuring tongues out, poop, a middle finger, rolling eyes, angry face, or, even worse, the aubergine! Remember that your comments on articles and blog posts can often be found in search engines.

Case study: Social media guru Gary Vee

Serial entrepreneur Gary Vee is a multimillionaire businessman and social media marketing guru who has founded at least 20 businesses. He's a pioneer in internet marketing and an influencer in the world of wine, NFTs and business in general. A household name in the US, he has many roles, including chairman and CEO of VaynerMedia, the digital marketing and communications agency he founded with his brother in 2009, which provides social media and strategy services to Fortune 500 companies. He has published more than a dozen

Building your profile online

books, in which he shares the secrets of his work. He started his career as an entrepreneur selling lemonade on the roadside in New Jersey aged six, and started his internet career as a teenager with the creation of a website for a small wine store founded by his father, who immigrated to the US from Belarus when Gary was three. His podcast, YouTube channel and Twitter account all have three or four million subscribers each and he has more than ten million followers on Instagram. Gary has posted plenty of videos on YouTube that share practical advice on using social media to build businesses. He advises that LinkedIn is number one for B2B – businesses selling products and services to other businesses – followed by YouTube, Facebook and X.

For businesses with products to sell to young people, TikTok is the best vehicle, followed by Instagram. Gary has many great content ideas and points out that some people are better at writing than making videos, so if you're not comfortable with making videos of yourself, you can do something simple such as posting static images on Instagram and writing about what the picture means to you. For example, if you were in New York for the weekend, you could take a photo of something and write about it. He says you could write to create curiosity. For example: 'I've been to New York seven times, but I've never been down this street. You could take a photo of anything – a banana, a car, a tree, a bird, your backyard. You really could take a photo of almost anything and then write three or four paragraphs that are very thoughtful about a point you're trying to make. Now, all of a sudden, you don't need a video and editing team. You could do it all by yourself.' One of Gary's best-known sayings is: 'Always think big. Never limit your thinking. Always remember the big picture.' This philosophy has certainly worked for him, and he's worth following if you want ideas on how to get the most out of your social media posts.

Posting your best pictures

In 2017, Victoria Beckham was criticised for asking a fan to retake a picture with her. She didn't like the first shot that he took, so she asked him to move with her into a room where the light was better – and three more shots were taken. Only then did she pick the best shot for him to use. Fussy? I don't think so. As a celebrity, Victoria realises she needs to protect her image and anything that doesn't come up to her high standards could be shared and criticised. Also, the only reason we know about this is because the self-confessed Spice Girls superfan in the pictures with her was a journalist who wrote all this up in *The Guardian*'s *Weekend* magazine. Victoria knew he was interviewing her for a wider audience and therefore was right to be careful about the photos. However, even if he was just an ordinary fan posting on his personal social media, the photo could have been reposted by someone else and gone viral.

At least she didn't go as far as legendary star Barbra Streisand, who takes no chances with her image in the visual economy. According to Matthew Belloni of online magazine *Puck*, after receiving a lifetime achievement award at the Screen Actors Guild Awards in February 2024, she had a person stand next to her at the after-party with a torch. This was pointed at anyone trying to get a photo of Streisand in order to ruin their shots. Belloni described this tactic as 'next-level dedication to vanity' (Boshoff 2024).

Even for the rest of us ordinary mortals, taking care over the pictures you post is essential. For example, when you're attending an event and in a bit of a rush to take photos and get them posted, always take several photos to choose from. Also, take care that your selfie is appropriate. The first-ever papal selfie was taken by some teenagers visiting the Vatican in 2013. Their photo image with Pope Francis went viral and was accepted as part of modern life. However, in the same year, the then prime minister of Denmark, Helle Thorning-Schmidt, faced criticism for inappropriate behaviour when she took a selfie together with UK prime minister David Cameron and US president Barack Obama while they were attending the memorial service for Nelson Mandela in Johannesburg, South Africa. Although she didn't post the selfie and told the media 'It isn't a particularly good picture', a press photographer had snapped the three political leaders looking very jolly together while she was taking it, so there was criticism of their attitude at a memorial service.

Selfies matter

Posting selfies isn't showing off – they demonstrate that you're out and about. This means that getting selfies right is important. You need to practise taking them correctly. So many people get the angle or the eyeline wrong by not looking at the lens of their phone's camera, or they post a shot with their mouth open and eyes closed. This is not a good look. Having a wide shot so that people can see relevant background is also crucial. There's no point in taking shots of yourself and your teeth in close-up at an event without showing something behind you that illustrates that you're somewhere interesting or exciting. You should also take general shots to illustrate your posts. It's the event, not you, that's the most important thing.

British supermodel Rosie Huntington-Whiteley was once quoted as saying she takes more than 150 pictures to get the right selfie to post online. This is one extreme of the selfie debate and you may not feel you need to go that far. However, taking at least ten shots of yourself and general shots of the event should give you a good choice. It's useful if, before you go to an event, you prepare by thinking about what pictures you want to take and of whom, and plan how and when you're going to take them.

Case study: Kim Kardashian, queen of the selfie

Probably the most extreme proponent of selfies is, not surprisingly, the ultimate selfie queen, Kim Kardashian. On a four-day day trip to Mexico with her family in 2016, she revealed that she took 6,000 selfies. During the trip, she combined business and pleasure by filming for her family's reality TV series, *Keeping Up with the Kardashians*, posing for a swimwear shoot and playing with her family on the beach and elsewhere. She gave her activities in Mexico intriguing titles such as 'beach hangs' and 'bikini tennis'. A journalist for *Refinery 29* worked out that Kim's epic selfie total was 1,500 shots per day using photo bursts, so she tried this out herself and concluded after just one day of taking 1,501 shots of herself that it's a lot harder than Kim makes it look.

It's important to recognise that Kardashian-style mega influencers are not the norm. If you want to be an influencer, even on a smaller scale, you have to work out whether you have the time to be able to dedicate yourself to this role and whether it will be profitable for you. Being an influencer is one of the ultimate uses of the visual economy. It's a way to build business using all the skills revealed in this book. It's not for everyone, but, if done well, it can be a vital part of building a business.

Becoming an influencer

What exactly is an influencer? An influencer is a social media personality who influences their audience to purchase particular products or services. They use their platform and their visual economy skills to provide their audiences with content that leverages their personal brand to give advice, offer promotions and answer questions. According to digital agency Moburst (Ailion 2023), there are five types of influencer, based on their number of followers:

- nano influencers: 0K–10K followers
- micro influencers: 10K–100K followers
- mid influencers: 100K–500K followers
- macro influencers: 500K–1M followers
- mega macro influencers: 1M+ followers.

Getting started as an influencer

If you want to be an influencer, you need to research your markets on different social media platforms, and they all provide information on how to do this. On Instagram, you don't need millions of followers. If you have only a few hundred or a few thousand followers, you can still livestream on the platform. Many people sell a lot of products on TikTok, so if you want to get started you can get advice in the form of free online courses from the grandly named TikTok University. You need to have at least a thousand followers on TikTok to get started as an influencer – but it's not all about followers; it's the engagement that matters. Engagement shows that they have a relationship with you and your brand that could lead to making money from sales or ads.

TikTok is big business

Plenty of young people aged 24 and under look at TikTok every day, so brands are keen to reach this audience. This is the visual economy at a fast pace. TikTok isn't just fun and games and lifestyle hacks – it's big business. The platform, owned by ByteDance, has experienced rapid growth since it launched in China in September 2016, where it's known as Douyin. It grew quickly in China and soon spread abroad. TikTok has grown from being a short-form video sharing platform with lots of people lip-syncing and dancing into a fully-fledged video service, with content of interest to a wide range of audiences and claiming 1.5 billion monthly active users in 2023 in more than 150 markets and 75 languages. Selling products direct to consumers via their mobiles is now a huge part of its business model, which generated an estimated $9.4 billion in revenue in 2022, a 100 per cent increase year on year.

TikTok is very different from LinkedIn. Look at all the different social media platforms to decide which of them best suit you and your business. It's worth noting that TikTok has been banned in some countries, including India (for engaging in activities prejudicial to the sovereignty and integrity of India after a deadly border clash between Indian and Chinese military forces), Afghanistan (for being not consistent with Islamic laws) and Somalia (for allegedly promoting terrorism). Several countries, including the UK and the US, have banned government employees from using TikTok on official phones and computers citing cybersecurity concerns about the platform's owner having links to the Chinese government. At the time of writing Western concerns over TikTok continue to grow – but even if the platform were to be fully banned, other short video platforms such as YouTube Shorts will no doubt fill the gap – and the general principles in this book about shooting good videos and using social media wisely will still be of great importance.

Know your audience

It's important to know your audience, what they want and what you can offer them. To be a successful influencer you need to decide on your niche. Before you start planning your content, you should familiarise yourself with other influencers on the platform you want to use. You need to have a passion for what you're talking about, so you can be authentic and be able to generate ideas. An influencer must stay in the minds of their followers, which means it's vital to post new content every day. To do this successfully you need to plan your content well ahead of time and record at least two weeks' worth of content in one session. This saves time but takes a lot of planning and organising, so once you start you can't stop.

Maintaining your presence on TikTok is 'like a full-time job'

Here's the view from the TikTok frontline from the singer/songwriter Paloma Faith. She revealed in an interview with *Waitrose* magazine (Kirkley 2024) that being on TikTok, where she promotes not only her music but her interiors brand Paloma Home to her more than half a million followers, is very demanding. With her typical frankness, at the start of the interview she apologised for arriving late. 'I'm really sorry,' she said. 'I've been lost in the weird vortex of TikTok. It's like a full-time job. I keep having to change outfits – I don't have enough time to do them every day, so I have to pretend.' Paloma also has more than three quarters of a million followers on Instagram to keep happy or, in her case, sad as well as so many of her songs are about divorce and getting rid of your man!

All the advice given in the next chapter about how to produce your videos professionally applies to creating settings for your images and videos. Many of the most successful influencers are selling beauty, fashion and fitness products, and diet plans. There are agencies that can help you to become a successful influencer and many brands prefer to use these to contact influencers. You need to be really sure that this is the right path for you and that you can sustain interest in yourself and your messages. If you're not passionate and knowledgeable about your topic, then this won't work for you.

Case study: Mrs Hinch cleans up

It's not only fashion, beauty and diets that can lead to success as an influencer. Cleaning and decluttering tips have both been extremely popular in recent years, and one big British success on Instagram is Sophie Hinchcliffe, better known by her brand name, Mrs Hinch. Speaking on ITV's *This Morning* in 2019, the glamorous former hairdresser from Essex said: 'I started a home account on Instagram purely to upload photos of my interiors and my home. And then one day I thought, let's clean on my stories, make it a little bit fun, quirky. And from there it's just rocketed.' After launching her cleaning hacks online, she gathered more than one million followers in just three months and her popularity keeps on growing. *The Daily Mail* reported that, between 2020 and 2023, she earned £7 million through her books, TV work and social media posts (Parkin 2023).

Hinch products are stocked in supermarkets as well as the Mrs Hinch shop on Amazon and she promotes her lifestyle and products on Instagram to her (at the time of writing) 4.8 million followers. Her books have been on the bestseller lists and she's credited with hugely increasing sales of many brands, including Zoflora, whose factory had to double production; Vileda, where sales of spray mops rocketed by 98 per cent; and Unilever, where sales of its Cif stainless steel cleaner have gone up by two thirds, thanks to her. However, Mrs Hinch has created a business that sells not just cleaning products but also make-up, clothes, bedding and household utensils, and in 2021 ratings site GoCompare listed her as the highest-paid 'homefluencer' in the UK, and second highest in the world.

So how has she done it? As well as her home cleaning clips, Mrs Hinch provides insights into her family life with husband Jamie and their sons Ronnie and Lennie. She has shared her diagnosis of autism and created a community of 'Hinchers' or the 'Hinch Army' who follow her on Instagram, Facebook and TikTok. These steps might seem trivial, but fanbase names make followers feel more like a community. Playing around with brand slogans and campaigns can really help build and solidify an influencer's brand identity, and Mrs Hinch and her fans regularly use specific hashtags such as #homehinchhome to reinforce this.

According to the experts at Influencer Update, her success boils down to trust. Her followers respect her authenticity and this is demonstrated by her organic follower count and high engagement rate on social media. I'd put Mrs Hinch's success down to hard work and the fact that she knows what she's doing and does it very well. Posting on Instagram in 2024, she said: 'People assume I am obsessed with cleaning; the truth is I'm not. I clean because it's my therapy. It helps me feel in control. I feel I have accomplished something each day, it frees my mind from overthinking and worrying. In fact, cleaning changed my life – 4.6 million followers later, forever grateful for you all. Thank you.'

A word of warning to would-be influencers

It's not easy to make money as an influencer and it's the Wild West out there. There are no rules about how much influencers should be paid and people who have built up thousands of followers have posted online complaining about the problems they've encountered in making money. Many have posted on Instagram about how some brands are unwilling to pay for posts and reels, offering only a few products, sometimes worth less than £100, in return for days' or even a week's worth of promotional work. You can find out more about this by checking out posts on @influencerpaygap on Instagram. While it's true that some influencers have made a good living from establishing themselves on social media, there are thousands more who have made very little money and have been poorly treated by brands both large and small. Try to secure a contract before you send anyone any of your promotional work. However, some brands are only looking for a cheap way to achieve more sales. In some cases, they are undercutting professional photographers and stylists by using nano influencers to produce content for their social media and websites and paying them little or nothing. The dilemma for nano influencers is whether to take product-only deals at the start in order to build up their followers or hold out for paid contracts.

Being an influencer is not for everyone. It's a big commitment in terms of time and being willing to share personal information to engage your followers and make them think of you as a trusted friend. You should study and analyse influencers you admire to see whether you'd be willing to share as much as they do. Being an influencer can be financially rewarding but it isn't automatic and to succeed you have to work hard and be sure it's something you really like doing, or it just won't work for you.

Livestreaming

This means speaking to your audience live online and is a great opportunity to showcase your products and services and have a conversation in real time with your audience/clients/potential clients. It's quite daunting for many people to speak live in this way and isn't something that everybody can do. If you have big fears about public speaking this may not suit you. However, if you're what broadcasters call 'a good talker' and are keen to speak in public about your business or organisation, you'll already have the skills to do this. In order to do your best, you'll need to plan ahead and rehearse what you want to say. You need to know your beginning, middle and end, as advised in Chapter 5. All the advice I give early in this chapter about background, lighting, framing, clothes etc, applies to livestreaming and you need to be sure that you're ticking all of these boxes at least an hour before you start. You also need to be sure that your internet connection is stable. Be prepared. Worrying about details at the last minute won't help you to perform well live. You can make some notes in big print that you can glance at while you're talking or put a sticky note on the side of your screen with a couple of important bullet points.

Always start on time and remember that people watching on replay will want you to get to your key message as soon as possible. Be conversational – say hello to people as they join and reply to comments and questions. Make sure you reinforce your call to action at the beginning and the end of your livestream and at least once if you do a Q&A session. If anything goes wrong, smile, own it and don't be embarrassed or collapse. Your audience are getting to know you and they understand that livestreaming is demanding. Provided you handle it well, you can get past anything that goes wrong. If you start livestreaming regularly, it's important to do so at least once a week. TikTok will close your LIVE room if they detect that you're an inactive host. Check each platform for the best length to go for. TikTok, Instagram, Facebook and LinkedIn all have useful instructions about going live and TikTok has a 'Get discovered' feature that will help you build your audience.

And finally...

You should always be careful about the content you post on social media. Take the time to think about what you're posting and commenting on from all angles. Second guessing yourself and asking a colleague or colleagues for their opinions is worthwhile. For example, you may have an opinion that you, your friends and colleagues don't think is controversial, but if you put it into a post, will there be lots of people who disagree with you and suddenly see you as biased and not someone they want to follow. If you're going for a niche market and don't think this matters, then go ahead. But always remember that if you go too far into a niche, it can become a tomb with no good future prospects!

Your social media content checklist

- ✦ Keep your social media profiles updated.
- ✦ Establish clear and measurable objectives for your posts and blogs.
- ✦ Define your target audience and what interests them.
- ✦ Check your competitors' social media – what's good and what's not?
- ✦ Draw up a calendar with a minimum of one post per week.
- ✦ Write a monthly blog, put it on your website and promote it.
- ✦ Define who will create posts and who will check them.
- ✦ Look into using automated scheduling.
- ✦ Use static images or videos for every post.
- ✦ Create photos – including selfies – in a professional style.
- ✦ Consider creating your own videos for posts.
- ✦ Invest in a ring light.
- ✦ Invest in a lapel mic.
- ✦ Investigate what AI can do for you.
- ✦ Always respond to your audience's comments or messages.
- ✦ Keep on top of your analytics – analyse total responses weekly in terms of views, enquiries and business gained.
- ✦ Consider whether regular webinars will be useful to you.
- ✦ Investigate livestreaming and its pros and cons for your business.

✦ Don't forget to Google yourself every week and if you don't come up on the first page for your name or your business, do some SEO (search engine optimisation) work to change this. Google has plenty of advice on how to do this.

Chapter 10

A glimpse into the metaverse

What is the metaverse and why is Mark Zuckerberg so keen on it that, in October 2021, he renamed Facebook's holding company Meta? Will the metaverse be the future of business and take over from the internet? Since the launch of Meta, sources at the company have said that they don't expect the metaverse to take off for at least another 10 to 15 years. However, although the metaverse may not be advancing as fast into business use as AI, it's still set to be part of the visual future that we will all take part in.

Mark Zuckerberg, aware of critics who have said that he appears to be concentrating more on AI and the even more sophisticated AGI (artificial general intelligence), said in a 2024 interview that he is committed to developing the metaverse with Meta spending more than $15 billion a year on this. 'I don't know how to more unequivocally state that we're continuing to focus on Reality Labs and the metaverse,' he said. He made it clear he sees a future in which virtual worlds are generated by AI and filled with AI characters that accompany real people and can be used across Meta's social apps, Facebook, Instagram and

Threads. He sees the metaverse as 'building the future of connection'. (Heath 2024)

How does the metaverse work?

The metaverse combines various technologies, including augmented reality (AR), virtual reality (VR) and artificial intelligence (AI) to create an immersive digital experience. The word metaverse comes from the 1992 science fiction novel *Snow Crash* by Neal Stephenson. It describes a place where physical, virtual and augmented realities converge to create 3D virtual reality spaces. These are interlinked, persistent and shared. This means the metaverse removes physical geographies and creates 'new land' with multiple, even infinite, geographies.

The word 'persistent' is key. When you take your headset off and leave the metaverse, it persists. It's continuous, and you miss out on events when you're not there. If you want to take it seriously, you can buy a 'persistent avatar'. This gives you the same avatar no matter which part of the metaverse you enter. These concepts are already familiar to the more than 350 million people who play Fortnite, a game that has created an immersive virtual world experience that's also a social meeting place for different groups of friends. The game also hosts non-gaming events and concerts.

Zuckerberg has said that the metaverse will be the successor to the mobile internet: 'We'll be able to feel present – like we're right there with people, no matter how far apart we actually are.' (Heath 2024) However, it's important to understand that the metaverse is not joined up like the internet. It's currently like a series of walled gardens – closed ecosystems where you have to register to enter, and each separate space wants you to stay in it and not go to other ones. This contrasts with the internet, which was established as a worldwide, not-for-profit, collaborative endeavour and was free to access right from the start.

According to a report by the management consultancy Markets and Markets, the global metaverse market was worth approximately $83.9 million in 2023 and is projected to grow to more than $1.3 billion by 2030, based mainly on the growth of global entertainment and gaming. Goldman Sachs has predicted the metaverse economy will eventually be worth trillions of dollars every year.

As an example of the effectiveness of the metaverse in generating income, the singer Ariana Grande earned $20 million doing five concerts using an avatar in different time zones on Fortnite. 'She' was viewed by more than 12 million people plus many more who watched recordings. Abba's smash-hit show *Abba Voyage* uses digital avatars at the specially built Abba Arena in London, and other shows using celebrity avatars are in the pipeline. These shows use technology developed for the metaverse and allow the audience to view and enjoy the avatars without wearing headsets.

Currently, the bulk of mass-market use of the metaverse has been in gaming, entertainment and pornography, which means that businesses outside these fields have only recently begun to take it seriously. However, many companies are now realising how useful metaverse simulated environments can be for marketing and brand awareness and for tasks such as onboarding, legal services, manufacturing, rehabilitation and training. This includes medical training, which is allowing surgeons to practise surgical techniques in a 3D virtual environment. Digital twinning, which can be used for the development and design of new products, is also being used to predict possible problems and advances by 'building' vastly complicated models of real-life projects such as factories.

Tourism and the metaverse

Some commentators predict that the metaverse will revolutionise the tourism and travel industry. How will it do this? The metaverse can provide detailed and realistic virtual travel experiences to inspire tourists before they book a holiday. With advanced VR and AR technologies, customers can explore destinations from the comfort of their homes and decide where they want to go and what they want to see in real life using the high-quality graphics and immersive environments the metaverse offers. They can walk through historic cities or the countryside, or even dive into the deep sea to explore marine life without leaving their living rooms. The metaverse can also play a vital role in preserving cultural heritage. Ancient cultural sites and monuments which are at risk from the wear and tear of too many visiting tourists can be safeguarded through digital replication and preservation in the metaverse for future generations to visit virtually.

The care industry and the metaverse

Developments in metaverse tourism are being keenly studied by the care industry, which is interested in using metaverse experiences for improving the lives of older people. For example, the metaverse can enable them to 'travel' to faraway places on their bucket lists when travel in real life might be too strenuous. They can also use the metaverse to reduce isolation and connect with others, continue lifelong learning and exercise. This can include a range of options tailored to their specific needs, including low-impact workouts, chair exercises, yoga sessions or guided walks through picturesque landscapes. They can walk on treadmills and keep fit while exploring a metaverse landscape. According to Melissa Powell (2024), the executive vice president and COO of Genesis HealthCare, a major US provider of senior care, 'The metaverse represents a paradigm shift in the way we approach senior care – fusing together technological innovation and human-centric care. Its potential to empower, engage and enhance the lives of older adults is profound, and this cannot be ignored. While it might still sound like a futuristic concept, its integration into senior care is here, and there are already a number of ways the metaverse is benefiting seniors. Through collaborative innovation and a shared vision for compassionate care, we can usher in a new era where the metaverse becomes a standard in the senior care industry for years to come.'

Case study: Wales is an anti-racist country

The metaverse has a lot of potential for use in education and, in 2022, the Welsh government became the first to announce that it was committed to ensuring Wales will be an anti-racist country by 2030. A crucial part of its Anti-Racist Wales Action Plan has been to develop an anti-racist curriculum in the form of a metaverse – the first anti-racist virtual world. This innovative project, led by Cardiff and Vale College on behalf of the Welsh government, provides an immersive learning

> experience developed and produced in collaboration with ethnic minority experts from schools, colleges, universities and third parties.

Metaverse disadvantages

The metaverse requires a lot of bandwidth and expensive and not terribly comfortable kit such as headsets and haptic gloves. The energy use is considerable and there has been a lot of criticism about this by climate change campaigners. Unlike the internet, the metaverse is hard to access while on the move. However, the kit is improving and constantly becoming cheaper so it's clear that accessing the metaverse will almost certainly get easier. Devices will get smaller and 5G will improve connectivity. For example, Samsung is already working on an augmented-reality contact lens, Apple has developed its first mixed-reality headset and Sony is also developing its own version. Announcing this in January 2024, Sony chief technology officer Yoshinori Matsumoto said the metaverse could follow a similar path to the world wide web and eventually become 'essential for our lives' as more people begin to use it (Landi 2024).

The new Sony mixed reality headset and controller system is aimed at businesses and creators, enabling them to do 3D design work using the headset, with virtual items appearing in front of the user's eyes and able to be manipulated using companion finger and hand controllers. Think Tom Cruise and the film *Minority Report*. However, Matsumoto acknowledged that the metaverse is still in its infancy and convincing people to use it 'heavily depends on the application or the content'. He added that Sony was already working with creators to 'make the metaverse valuable when you arrive'.

Another big disadvantage is that there's almost no regulation in the metaverse. Decentraland, an early metaverse platform, was intended to create a digital, decentralised democracy, but this is an exception. In most of the metaverse there are no laws, so there's no copyright protection and no legal redress for thefts or damage. There's currently no redress for crime in the metaverse, including sexual assaults and rape, which, because of the immersive nature of the experience, victims have described as being just as emotionally damaging as attacks in the real world (Waugh 2024).

Metaverse advantages

The metaverse is limitless – in other words, there's no limit on the number of metaverses that can be created. Given the immersive nature of the metaverse, there are huge advantages for marketers who'll have the opportunity to collect unprecedentedly detailed data about consumers. When you put on your headset and enter a virtual world, everything you do is tracked. For marketing professionals, the future is no longer just about fighting for eyeballs but is as detailed as actually tracking eye movements.

Big brands are now buying 'properties' in the metaverse. McDonald's has announced that customers will be able to order its takeaway food and get real food delivered to their door. Brands that have created their own metaverses include Meta, Microsoft, Disney, Louis Vuitton and Coca-Cola. Luxury brands are partnering with existing metaverse platforms and selling clothes for avatars as well as humans. According to Burberry's global VP for innovation, Rachel Waller, the metaverse is the 'new frontier of storytelling', which will allow brands to engage with customers in a way that they haven't been able to before. Burberry, a British luxury fashion brand founded in 1856, made its name making classic country clothing. Over a century later, Burberry collaborated with Minecraft on a capsule collection designed 'to bring checks and trench coats to The Overworld', and the company has worked with Mythical Games since 2021 with its best-known game being Blankos Block Party.

Other fashion brands, including Gucci, Ralph Lauren, Vans, Forever 21 and Nike, have collaborated with Roblox, a gaming platform with more than 50 million users a day. Each brand has its own game world within the Roblox interconnected metaverse and uses the same currency. Hyundai World also partnered with Roblox. Nike's collaboration with the metaverse platform RTFKT allows it to sell expensive limited editions of its shoes. Shoes that only avatars can wear can cost hundreds of dollars. Luxury brand Maison Valentino has partnered with Meta to enable people to dress their avatars on Meta platforms. As reported by *Vogue* magazine, these include Instagram, Facebook, Messenger and Meta virtual reality experiences, with branded looks inspired by Valentino's collections.

Decentraland features some of the world's biggest superstars and brands, including Morgan Stanley, Coca-Cola, Adidas, Samsung and Snoop Dogg. Gamers who aren't so interested in luxury fashion can design football shirts for their avatars. There are numerous online stores offering clothing for avatars and digital fashion is already worth hundreds of millions of pounds a month to gaming platforms. Other big brands trading in the metaverse include Christie's and Sotheby's. These auction houses are selling digital art through NFTs – non-fungible tokens. NFTs are unique tokens that authenticate the art and exist in a decentralised 'blockchain'. Big brands have recognised that building an immersive brand experience, especially with young audiences accustomed to gaming, has huge advantages.

Where does this leave small businesses?

Mark Zuckerberg and Meta have produced an AI product called 'Builder Bot', which allows users to create their own basic virtual world. A growing number of metaverse development companies can help businesses try out the metaverse for themselves, whether it's creating or being part of games, or running events. For smaller businesses, purchasing land and property in the metaverse can be too expensive. If you're interested in buying a plot in Decentraland, you're looking at spending at least $10,000, while the most expensive plots sell for more than $1 million. You also have to purchase land, goods and services using MANA, Decentraland's own cryptocurrency. What's clear is that the metaverse is massive for gamers and experts predict that the gamification of brands, as already exploited by Burberry and others, will increase and creating worlds with augmented reality and games around brands will be profitable. Using the metaverse for education and training is also a growing trend and metaverse experts predict that virtual reality meetings may also become part of our visual future.

The metaverse is often described as the next big thing that the internet will evolve into. But what does this mean for businesses in practical terms? There are many potential training and industrial applications for the metaverse. Research by Nokia shows that the technology is already being successfully used for training, meetings and events, marketing, medical operations, health and safety, factory production and logistics.

Case study: Nokia Learning Space

One of the clearest and most widely applicable uses for metaverse technologies is training. Virtual reality can bring people together without the expense and downtime associated with travelling to a central training location. It's a strategy that Nokia has been employing since 2021, when they began to see VR as a natural progression from bringing people together using videoconferencing. While training on videoconference can be quite one way, VR makes learning a more practical, hands-on experience.

Gilberto Serra, head of digitalisation at Nokia People Services, has led the development of the Nokia Learning Space, a VR training environment built with a 3D engine for developing video games. 'It's a creative room where people can learn under the guidance of an instructor,' Serra explains. The first program we delivered was to learn how to install Nokia equipment. Participants go through the whole process, from unpacking the equipment to attaching the power cable, mounting it in the rack, switching it on and installing the software. And they get their certification at the end.' Nokia also runs a 30-minute VR-only weekly learning session: a metaverse update of the 'lunch and learn' concept already used at many companies. Unlike desk-top-based videoconferencing applications, this is a much more immersive experience. Participants use VR headsets and see other participants as avatars, while the presenter's hologram has real facial expressions and movements. As 5G-Advanced networks roll out, Serra says, full 3D holograms can be projected onto AR glasses so that participants will really feel as if they are all in the room together.

Case study: Virtual services for hands-on work

One very powerful use case for AR is the provision of virtual guidance for people faced with technically challenging hands-on tasks, such as rescue workers, field technicians or firefighters. Virtual overlays can provide them with vital information on what to look for, where to focus, and how to complete their tasks successfully. Bosch, for instance, has developed an AR application that guides its after-market workshops on how to perform specialist maintenance and repair tasks on vehicles, such as readjusting driver assistance sensors after replacing the windscreen. It estimates that guided assistance like this can reduce the time taken to carry out certain tasks by as much as 15 per cent.

Futurist Bernard Marr (2022) says that the metaverse offers sustainability benefits as well as better ways to network and collaborate. 'Pre-pandemic, I was getting on a 12-hour flight to deliver a half-hour keynote, then flying 12 hours back,' he told a Nokia podcast. 'You can do this online today. And there are no limitations in terms of audience. There's no impact on the environment, so it is better all around.'

Get ready for more revolution to come

The case studies above show that the metaverse is no longer something we're heading towards. It's here today and already delivering practical benefits such as lower costs, faster time to market and a greater sense of inclusion. And many businesses are waking up to these opportunities. Two thirds of the B2B companies surveyed by Nokia said they're currently educating themselves about its possibilities, while 5 per cent revealed themselves as early adopters, already investing in metaverse technologies and expertise.

With new use cases emerging all the time and the enabling technologies of the metaverse rapidly evolving, it may not be long until AR glasses are as ubiquitous in the workplace as notebook computers and smartphones are today. For enterprises that want to be ready for the metaverse revolution around the corner, the time to start planning is now.

So, in the future could we all end up living in the metaverse and communicating using our avatars, as in the Bruce Willis film *Surrogates*? The film was released in 2009 and now that the metaverse and AI are really getting going, it doesn't seem so much like science fiction anymore, does it? More recently, in 2018, the film *Ready Player One* was released. Set in 2045, it tackled the theme of people living in a multiplayer virtual reality entertainment universe and was a big hit, grossing more than $600 million worldwide. Although even the most optimistic experts predict that we're still years away from avatar living as an everyday norm, when Mark Zuckerberg is backing the metaverse with billions of dollars every year, and businesses are already using it for marketing, tourism, training and HR functions, it could be with us as a vital part of the visual economy much sooner than we expect.

Chapter 11

The future of the visual economy

If you want to succeed in the visual economy, it's essential to recognise that you need to acquire and develop visual skills to enable you to look and sound professional. You need to understand visual grammar. Whether it's posting images and videos on social media, looking smart in online meetings, making and presenting videos, designing visually attractive presentations, giving media interviews, podcasting or entering the metaverse, you need to keep on learning and keep up to date.

Artificial intelligence is a game changer and there's clearly a long way to go before we see all the effects of how it will operate in the visual economy. AI will have a massive impact on all organisations, enabling everyone to reduce their time on repetitive tasks – and it has arrived at a time when economic pressures mean that businesses are under pressure to cut costs. Because AI supports cost efficiency, it can enable workplaces to accomplish more with less, an advantage for organisations of all sizes.

On the other hand, there are disadvantages. People are already creating deepfakes and shallowfakes (fake images and video created without using AI) and celebrities are particularly vulnerable. The first-known examples of deepfake videos, posted to Reddit in 2017, featured celebrities' faces swapped with those of porn stars. Since then, stars such as Taylor Swift, Tom Cruise and others have been deepfaked for non-pornographic reasons. The man who put Tom Cruise's face onto his own is actor and businessman Miles Fisher, known as DeepTomCruise. In interviews he has said he has always had a lot of people tell him he looks like Cruise, so he decided to lean into this and 'for a joke' he used AI to deepfake the actor. He claims to be astonished that he built a following on TikTok of 5.2 million people. He has used this fame to publicise his company Metaphysics, an AI company he describes as the future of 'synthetic storytelling'.

Miles Fisher says he began being DeepTomCruise '… with the purpose of generating awareness for manipulated media, and the potential for what could happen. Obviously [DeepTomCruise] is kind of irreverent, fun, entertaining content. When it suddenly blew up we contacted Tom Cruise's team and ultimately they didn't have an issue.' (Young 2023)

Tom Cruise hasn't commented on his deepfakes, and it's all very jolly for Miles Fisher and his businesses, but where does it leave the rest of us in terms of trust in what we see online? Politicians are concerned that deepfake images and videos are damaging trust and spreading disinformation during elections and can cause damage to democracy. Deepfake videos that appear to feature politicians, including Joe Biden, Barack Obama and Donald Trump, have gone viral since the technology emerged in 2017. Deepfakes are able to place politicians, celebrities or indeed anyone into an image or a video they never participated in, making them appear to do or say things that never happened. Governments are concerned about AI fakery in politics and also about how AI is being used by people who want to shame and harass others, especially women. Interpol lists the use of AI in a wide range of criminal activities. These include extortion and fraud, falsifying online identities, falsifying or manipulating electronic evidence for criminal justice investigations, online child sexual exploitation and non-consensual pornography.

What can be done to combat deepfakes?

Options being considered to combat deepfakes include the use of blockchain authentication for secure video storage because it uses systems that are decentralised and continuously verified and reverified by every entity that uses them (World Economic Forum 2021). This makes it nearly impossible to change information after it's been created. Some experts are predicting that in future recording devices will need to incorporate encrypted timestamps which act like watermarks to guarantee authenticity and re-establish trust in visual and audio media.

However, we're not there yet because currently software is available that can remove existing watermarks. In February 2024, Meta announced that it's developing more secure watermarks, although it admitted even after using the latest technology, it could still be possible for malicious agents to remove them (Holt 2024). The race is on to develop reliable AI detection tools.

Apart from software defences against malicious deepfakes, there are also some company registration schemes committing to ethical use of AI video technology.

Then there's lifelogging. This started out in 2001 as an experiment by computer experts trying to preserve a complete record of their lives by making a continuous record of their daily activities using digital devices or computer applications. Now some people are lifelogging using apps on smartphones and other digital devices to prevent themselves from being put into deepfake videos because they always have proof of where they are. Although some static AI images can be detected because of 'six finger' hands and other oddities, there's a race on between AI companies to improve AI image datasets by including, for example, more reference photos of hands with five fingers, so this will eventually get rid of the weird hands problem, and it will become more difficult to spot these fake images.

Despite the dark sides of AI, enthusiasts point out that it's offering endless possibilities for assisting both text and visual creativity and we need to learn to incorporate it into our work and everyday lives. Some workforce experts are predicting that as AI takes over many routine tasks, such as generating emails and reports, inputting and analysing data, thereby improving operational efficiency, it will be vital for workers to develop their soft skills, such as communication, empathy and collaboration. A *New York Times* headline in 2024 summed this up: 'When your technical skills are eclipsed, your humanity will matter more than ever'. The authors Aneesh Raman, LinkedIn's chief workforce expert, and Maria Flynn, president of Jobs for the Future, highlight the importance of a relationship economy and their belief that people skills and social abilities are going to become even more central to success than ever before (Raman & Flynn 2024).

Having recently spent an hour online trying to change my car insurance and finding my way constantly blocked by virtual assistants asking me questions irrelevant to my queries, then giving me useless answers and suddenly closing the chat or, when I had another go, telling me to wait (a long time) to speak to a 'customer specialist' (a human), I finally gave up and changed to another insurance provider. Half an hour of unhelpful virtual assistants followed by half an hour of muzak with repeated recorded messages telling me 'we really appreciate your patience and will be with you soon' did not make me willing to give this insurance company my money. Customer care and soft skills? AI doesn't have them. But you do. You have the skills to use the visual economy to build trusting relationships with your customers and clients.

Next steps

What will you try out first? How will you use your visual skills to improve your personal branding and your marketing? Will it be making your own videos and posting them online, upping your use of static images and video on social media platforms, livestreaming, podcasting, presenting online or in person, giving media interviews or even becoming an influencer? Or all of these? Whichever new skills you start to use, my goal throughout this book has been to provide you with the knowledge to recognise the importance of the visual revolution and make the best use of the visual economy.

Whether you're promoting your own business or highlighting the products and services of the organisation you work for, whether you are self-employed or working for a small, medium or large organisation, the facts and practical advice in this book should make your choices more informed and more effective in today's fast-changing world.

There are many exciting new prospects ahead as well as challenges. I hope this book has enabled you to understand the skillsets you require to succeed in the visual economy, and I wish you success in your career as a visual communicator. If you'd like to find out more about boosting your visual skills, my company TV News London Ltd has decades of valuable experience to share with you.

The immense power of the visual economy is in your hands. Good luck and I hope to work with you soon.

Acknowledgements

I've loved writing this book, but it has taken a lot of work and I'd like to thank my colleagues at TV News London, Malcolm Douglas and Lydia Nicolaides, for their understanding and assistance as I've toiled away at it. I would also like to thank Dr Annmarie Hanlon of Cranfield School of Management, Laura Hutchinson from Historic Royal Palaces, Lisa Gilbe from Style Stories, Lynne Parker, founder of Funny Women, Paul McEntee, CEO of Here Be Dragons, Tim Prizeman, RB Consulting, and Gina McAdam of Stratemarco Ltd for their assistance and encouragement.

Resources

Introduction

Howarth, J (2023) 'How many people own smartphones? (2024-2029)'. Exploding Topics, 14 December. URL: explodingtopics.com/blog/smartphone-stats

Feldman, B (2016) 'The vast majority of web content will be video, says man who can unilaterally make such a decision'. *NY Magazine*, 23 February. URL: nymag.com/intelligencer/2016/02/zuckerberg-video-will-be-most-of-the-web.html

Chapter 1

YouTube Creators: youtube.com/channel/UCkRfArvrzheW2E7b6SVT7vQ

Vimeo offers free as well as paid services: vimeo.com/upgrade-plan

Other subtitling and professional editing products:

- adobe.com/uk/products/premiere
- veed.io
- subtitlebee.com
- captionme.co.uk

Advice on making videos on your smartphone: iphoneographers.tv

AI resources:

- openai.com/chatgpt
- bing.com/create
- elevenlabs.io
- invideo.io
- pictory.ai
- rawshorts.com
- canva.com
- speechify.com

Chapter 2

Gant, J (2022) 'People in glass houses! Green campaigner lectures GMB viewers on damage that conservatories are doing to the planet – while sitting in her conservatory'. *Mail Online*, 20 January. URL: dailymail.co.uk/news/article-10421987/Green-campaigner-lectures-GMB-viewers-damage-conservatories-sitting-hers

Carroll, R (2020) 'Irish MEP Luke "Ming" Flanagan caught with no trousers in EU debate'. *The Guardian*, 3 June. URL: theguardian.com/world/2020/jun/03/irish-mep-luke-ming-flanagan-caught-with-no-trousers-in-eu-debate

Deegan, G (2020) 'GMIT spent €5,000 on report into lecturers insulting students on video call'. *Breakingnews.ie*, 11 July. URL: breakingnews.ie/reland/gmit-spent-e5000-on-report-into-lecturers-insulting-students-on-video-call-1333771.html

Usborne, S (2017) 'The expert whose children gatecrashed his TV interview'. *The Guardian*, 20 December. URL: theguardian.com/media/2017/dec/20/robert-kelly-south-korea-bbc-kids-gatecrash-viral-storm

O'Connor, R (2023) 'Sir Richard Branson's live TV interview interrupted by world's loudest cricket as viewers switch channels over noise'. *Metro*, 30 August. URL: metro.co.uk/2023/08/30/richard-bransons-live-tv-interview-interrupted-by-worlds-loudest-cricket-19416464

Baker, S (2021) '"We can see everything!" Mortified South African official apologises after his wife appears naked behind him during Zoom meeting on Covid crisis'. *Mail Online*, 1 April. URL: dailymail.co.uk/news/article-9427591/South-African-official-apologises-wife-appears-NAKED-Zoom-meeting

Chapter 3

Meikle, J (2014) 'Rosetta scientist Dr Matt Taylor apologises for "offensive" shirt'. *The Guardian*, 14 November. URL: theguardian.com/science/2014/nov/14/rosetta-comet-dr-matt-taylor-apology-sexist-shirt

Chapter 4

Free to view TED talks: TED.com

Anderson, C (2016) *TED Talks: The official TED guide to public speaking*. Houghton Mifflin Harcourt.

Canva's Visual Economy Report (2023): canvavisualeconomy.com

Guy Kawasaki's 10/20/30 rule of PowerPoint: guykawasaki.com/the_102030_rule

Christine Lagarde's talk: imf.org/en/News/Articles/2019/02/21/sp022819-md-the-financial-sector-redefining-a-broader-sense-of-purpose

'Chelsea Clinton says why she doesn't talk to the media': youtube.com/watch?v=XS1JbxuSbsU

Chapter 5

Newman, R (2021) 'Caught with his trousers down: Embarrassing moment Antwerp Mayor's wardrobe malfunction is exposed during an interview as an unfortunately placed mirror reveals his underwear'. *Mail Online*, 5 January. URL: dailymail.co.uk/news/article-9113791/Antwerp-Mayor-suffers-wardrobe-malfunction-caught-wearing-no-trousers-interview

BBC News (2018) 'Sainsbury's boss sorry for singing We're in the Money'. URL: bbc.co.uk/news/business-43959687

Rainsford, R (2024) 'Tucker Carlson: Putin takes charge as TV host gives free rein to Kremlin'. BBC News, 9 February. URL: bbc.co.uk/news/world-europe-68248740

Tapsfield, J (2023) 'He really is Greg HANDS! Tory chair is caught with notes scrawled on his palm as he tours TV studios amid local election battle'. *Mail Online*, 16 April. URL: dailymail.co.uk/news/article-11978421/Tory-chair-Greg-Hands-caught-interview-notes-scrawled-palm

Chapter 6

Jefferies, M (2022) 'Matt Hancock reveals sneaky "pivot" technique politicians use to avoid questions. *Daily Mirror*, 11 November. URL: mirror.co.uk/tv/tv-news/matt-hancock-reveals-sneaky-pivot-28471582

Lucy Frazer interview: news.sky.com/video/dig-lucy-frazer-mp-13053823

Chapter 7

Belcher, S (2021) 'The "Love Island" cast has been rocked by three suicides in the last year'. Distractify, 19 February. URL: distractify.com/p/love-island-deaths

Saner, E (2019) '"They sell you a dream": are reality shows such as Love Island failing contestants?' *The Guardian*, 3 June. URL: theguardian.com/tv-and-radio/2019/jun/03/they-sell-you-a-dream-are-reality-shows-such-as-love-island-failing-contestants

Chapter 8

Howarth, J (2024) 'How many podcasts are there? (New 2024 data)'. Exploding Topics. URL: explodingtopics.com/blog/number-of-podcasts

Wilson, C (2024) 'Joe Rogan's net worth as multi-million Spotify saw him become world's richest podcaster'. *Daily Express US*. URL: the-express.com/sport/mma/138168/Joe-Rogan-net-worth-podcast-ufc

Son, M (2023) 'The complete history of podcasts'. Descript, 30 November. URL: descript.com/blog/article/history-of-podcasts

Webster, T (2023) 'The podcast landscape'. Sounds Profitable, 30 August. URL: soundsprofitable.com/research/the-podcast-landscape

Makari, R (2023) 'One-third of UK adults are monthly podcast listeners, according to RAJAR survey'. Podpod, 23 October. URL: podpod.com/article/1845313/one-third-uk-adults-monthly-podcast-listeners-according-rajar-survey

Podcast resources:

- podcastindex.org
- thepodcasthost.com
- podmatch.com
- acast.com
- audacityteam.org
- riverside.fm
- podcastle.ai
- podbean.com

Ofcom podcast survey, April 2021: ofcom.org.uk/__data/assets/pdf_file/0027/217737/ofcom-podcast-survey-2021-technical-report.pdf

Podcast advertising worldwide: statista.com/outlook/dmo/digital-media/digital-music/podcast-advertising/worldwide

Romanoff, Z (2023) 'How much money do podcasts actually make?'. Descript, 2 November. URL: descript.com/blog/article/how-much-money-do-podcasts-actually-make

Lisa Gillbe: lisagillbestyle.com

Sernoff, R (2023) '15 best podcast hosting sites to help grow your audience'. Wix blog, 17 December. URL: wix.com/blog/podcast-hosting-sites

Chapter 9

Holloway, J (2013) *Personal Branding For Brits: How to promote yourself, raise your profile and get ahead... without sounding like an idiot.* Spark Ltd. URL: jennifer-holloway.co.uk/book

Garone, E (2014) 'Can social media get you fired?' BBC Worklife, 3 November. URL: bbc.com/worklife/article/20130626-can-social-media-get-you-fired

Smith, L (2017) 'British Council boss sacked for

calling Prince George symbol of "white privilege" denied payout'. *The Independent*, 7 November. URL: independent.co.uk/news/uk/home-news/council-boss-prince-george-white-privilege-comments-angela-gibbins-fired-compensation-a8041496.html

BBC News (2009) '"Lying down" NHS staff suspended'. 9 February. URL: news.bbc.co.uk/1/hi/8246197.stm

Quinn, B (2008) 'Virgin sacks 13 over Facebook "chav" remarks'. *The Guardian*, 1 November. URL: theguardian.com/business/2008/nov/01/virgin-atlantic-facebook

O'Carroll, L (2012) 'Rebekah Brooks: David Cameron signed off texts "LOL"'. *The Guardian*, 11 May. URL: theguardian.com/media/2012/may/11/rebekah-brooks-david-cameron-texts-lol

Gary Vee: garyvaynerchuk.com

Stone, J (2017) '"Oh, it's you!" said Geri: my quest to meet the Spice Girls'. *The Guardian*, 5 May. URL: theguardian.com/music/2017/may/05/my-quest-to-meet-the-spice-girls

Boshoff, A (2024) 'Hollywood icon Barbra Streisand takes no chances with her image'. *Mail Online* (down page story), 29 February. URL: dailymail.co.uk/tvshowbiz/article-13142933/Cancel-culture-Downton-Abbeys-Hugh-Bonneville-prepares-play-fallen-national-treasure-new-ITV-drama

Reilly, J (2013) 'The year of the "selfie": From pop stars to politicians, can ANYONE resist the narcissistic lure of the mobile phone self-portrait?' *Mail Online*, 27 December. URL: dailymail.co.uk/news/article-2524515/Top-20-selfies-year

Farley, R (2016) 'I tried to take 6,000 selfies like Kim K – & failed miserably'. *Refinery 29*, 27 October. URL: refinery29.com/en-us/2016/10/127081/copying-kim-kardashian-selfies

Ailion, J (2023) '4 types of influencers: which type do you need for your campaign?'. Moburst, 16 July. URL: moburst.com/blog/types-of-influencers

TikTok resources:

- getstarted.tiktok.com/gofulltiktok
- businessofapps.com/data/tik-tok-statistics
- mashable.com/article/tiktok-ban-countries
- newsweek.com/21-dangerous-tiktok-trends-that-have-gone-viral-1573734
- tiktok.com/creators/creator-portal/getting-started-on-tiktok/tiktok-university

Kirkley, P (2024) 'True faith'. Waitrose & Partners *Weekend* magazine, 15 February. URL: weekend-online.com/issue685/10/index.html

Parkin, L (2023) 'Mrs Hinch "earns an eye-watering £7million in just three years" from best-selling books, TV work and social media plugs'. *Mail Online*, 31 December. URL: dailymail.co.uk/tvshowbiz/article-12913591/Mrs-Hinch-7million-3-years

Cresswell, N (2020) 'Let's talk about Mrs Hinch – an in-depth "cleanfluencer" case study'. *Influencer Update*, 19 February. URL: influencerupdate.biz/feature/68498/lets-talk-about-mrs-hinch-an-in-depth-cleanfluencer-case-study

Influencer resources:

- instagram.com/influencerpaygap
- moburst.com/blog/how-to-build-the-right-influencer-campaign

Kesavalu, S (2024) 'What is live streaming? Meaning and how it works'. V Played, 8 February. URL: vplayed.com/blog/what-is-live-streaming

Chapter 10

Heath, A (2024) 'Mark Zuckerberg's new goal is creating artificial general intelligence'. The Verge, 18 January. URL: theverge.com/2024/1/18/24042354/mark-zuckerberg-meta-agi-reorg-interview

Landi, M (2024) 'Sony bets on metaverse with new mixed reality headset'. URL: independent.co.uk/tech/sony-apple-japanese-mark-zuckerberg-meta-b2476713.html

Immersive Learning News (2023) 'The metaverse: a gateway to cultural heritage and tourism'. 1 November. URL: www.immersivelearning.news/2023/11/01/the-metaverse-a-gateway-to-cultural-heritage-and-tourism

Powell, M (2024) 'The metaverse and its future-forward impact on senior care'. *McKnights Long Term Care News*, 12 February. URL: mcknights.com/blogs/guest-columns/the-metaverse-and-its-future-forward-impact-on-senior-care

Welsh Government Anti-Racism Metaverse: antiracism.wales

Clark, M (2022) 'NFTs, explained'. *The Verge*, 6 June. URL: theverge.com/22310188/nft-explainer-what-is-blockchain-crypto-art-faq

Valli, L N (2023) 'What is the role of NFT in the metaverse?' LinkedIn Pulse, 26 February. URL: linkedin.com/pulse/what-role-nft-metaverse-latha-narayanan-valli

Metaverse market report: marketsandmarkets.com/Market-Reports/metaverse-market-166893905.html

Wolfe, L (2023) '10 metaverse examples of brands doing it right'. Medium, 18 September. URL: medium.com/@lunawolfe01/10-metaverse-examples-of-brands-doing-it-right-241c10c55b5f

Young, H (2022) 'The metaverse: how should small businesses prepare?'. Startups, 18 December. URL: startups.co.uk/business-ideas/the-metaverse-for-small-businesses

Calma, J (2022) 'Here's how much energy crypto mining gobbles up in the US'. *The Verge*, 8 September. URL: theverge.com/2022/9/8/23341685/crypto-mining-bitcoin-energy-environment-impact-report-biden

Marr, B (2022) 'How luxury brands are making money in the metaverse'. *Forbes*, 19 January. URL: forbes.com/sites/bernardmarr/2022/01/19/how-luxury-brands-are-making-money-in-the-metaverse/?sh=177b281a5714

Marr, B (2022) 'The 10 best examples of the metaverse everyone should know about'. LinkedIn Pulse, 31 May. URL: linkedin.com/pulse/10-best-examples-metaverse-everyone-should-know-bernard-marr

MAD//Fest London (2022): 'The metaverse is the 'new frontier of storytelling' for brands'. Madfestlondon.com, 22 July. URL: madfestlondon.com/insights/burberry-metaverse-storytelling

Waugh, R (2024) 'I was "gang-raped" in the metaverse – the trauma was similar to a real-world assault'. *Mail Online*, 13 January. URL: dailymail.co.uk/sciencetech/

article-12948027/I-gang-raped-metaverse-trauma-similar-real-world-assault

PA Media (2024) 'Sony bets on metaverse with a new mixed reality headset'. *Mail Online*, 11 January. URL: dailymail.co.uk/wires/pa/article-12949677/Sony-bets-metaverse-new-mixed-reality-headset

McDowell, M (2023) 'Valentino to dress Meta avatars in digital fashion'. *Vogue Business*, 14 July. URL: voguebusiness.com/technology/valentino-to-dress-meta-avatars-in-digital-fashion

Metaverse development services: flipsidegroup.com/metaverse.html

Marr, B (2023) 'Virtual reality, real business: the impact of the metaverse on companies'. *Forbes*, 26 October. URL: forbes.com/sites/bernardmarr/2023/10/26/ervirtual-reality-real-business-the-impact-of-the-metaverse-on-companies

Nokia report: 'Six trailblazing use cases for the metaverse in business'. URL: nokia.com/metaverse/six-metaverse-use-cases-for-businesses

Chapter 11

Young, C (2023) 'How does Tom Cruise feel about those viral deepfakes of him getting up to shenanigans?' Cinema Blend. URL: cinemablend.com/movies/how-does-tom-cruise-feel-about-those-viral-deepfakes-of-him-getting-up-to-shenanigans

World Economic Forum (2021) 'Blockchain can help combat the threat of deepfakes. Here's how'. October 12. URL: weforum.org/agenda/2021/10/how-blockchain-can-help-combat-threat-of-deepfakes

Raman, A & Flynn, M (2024) 'When your technical skills are eclipsed, your humanity will matter more than ever'. *New York Times*, 14 February. URL: nytimes.

com/2024/02/14/opinion/ai-economy-jobs-colleges.html

Holt, K (2024) 'Meta plans to more broadly label AI-generated content'. URL: engadget.com/meta-plans-to-more-broadly-label-ai-generated-content-152945787.html

About the author

Roz Morris is the managing director and co-founder of TV News London Ltd – **tvnewslondon.co.uk** – and has been a leader in media training and presentation training for more than 25 years. This book builds on her extensive experience as a journalist and media trainer, working with hundreds of businesses, professional organisations, universities, museums, charities and NGOs, as well as authors and politicians in the UK and across the world, enabling them to excel in their external communications in videos, presentations and media interviews. She is a broadcaster who has recently appeared on Apple TV+, Paramount+, Talk TV, ITV's *This Morning*, and BBC Radio 4.

She is passionate about clear communications and making the most of visual skills. She says: 'Every time I give a media interview, make a presentation or present a video, I take my own advice and I'm glad to tell you it works. Every time!'

Roz started her career in journalism as a reporter for *The Guardian* and *The Observer*, where she was the youngest reporter on both newspapers, then moved into broadcasting as a reporter and presenter for BBC Radio 4's *World at One*, BBC Scotland, Tyne Tees TV, RTE (Radio

Telefis Eirann) and ITN. She was a freelance reporter for newspapers, magazines, radio and television, as well as a media trainer, while bringing up her family and now has four grandchildren. She regularly blogs about media issues and the visual economy, and you can contact her for information about her media training and presentation training services at **info@tvnewslondon.co.uk**

I have worked with Roz for many years, and she is the best in the business. She has helped us put our senior client teams through invaluable training ahead of appearances on live TV and radio. I definitely recommend her to anyone in need of top-notch media training.
   Paul McEntee, CEO, Here Be Dragons PR

I've been using Roz for media training for my clients and in house for more than 20 years. Strongly recommended.
   Tim Prizeman, director, R B Consulting and author, *The Thought Leadership Manual*

We have worked with Roz and the TV News London team on a number of occasions and have had excellent feedback from our senior spokespeople, with positive improvements in their media handling skills and confidence.
   Robert Blevin, head of external communications, University of Surrey

EU Safety Representative: euComply OÜ Pärnu mnt 139b-14 11317 Tallinn
Estonia hello@eucompliancepartner.com +33 756 90241

www.ingramcontent.com/pod-product-compliance
Lightning Source LLC
Chambersburg PA
CBHW040516220526
45473CB00012B/2881